PATHS ARE
MADE
BY WALKING

PATHS ARE MADE BY WALKING

PRACTICAL STEPS FOR ATTAINING SERENITY

THÉRÈSE JACOBS-STEWART

WARNER BOOKS

An AOL Time Warner Company

Warner Books, Inc., 1271 Avenue of the Americas, New York, NY 10020

Visit our Web site at www.twbookmark.com.

An AOL Time Warner Company

Printed in the United States of America

First Printing: June 2003
10 9 8 7 6 5 4 3 2 1

The Library of Congress Cataloging-in-Publication Data
Jacobs-Stewart, Thérèse.
    Paths are made by walking : practical steps for attaining serenity / Thérèse
Jacobs-Stewart.
        p. cm.
    Includes bibliographical references.
    ISBN 0-446-53067-0
    1. Peace of mind. 2. Spiritual exercises. 3. Peace of mind—Religious
aspects. I. Title.

BF637.P3 J33 2003
158—dc21   2002031147

Book design by Giorgetta Bell McRee

For Jimmy, the one whose heart beats with mine

ACKNOWLEDGMENTS

My heartfelt thanks to Daniel Schultz, my writing collaborator, whose creativity, diligence, and superb craftsmanship have made this book what it is. My gratitude extends to Elizabeth Marie Dorn, our concept consultant, for her valuable ideas and feedback along the way. And to Tom Blunt, a talented young artist from Mesa, Arizona, for conceptualizing the brain graphics depicted here.

To my spiritual teachers Father Michael Winterer, Sister Mary Sharon Riley, and Khenchen Thrangu Rinpoche, who have guided my path and opened my heart. To Dosho Port-sensei, for lending his insight and knowledge of ancient practices to this endeavor. And to Daniel Goleman, whose mentoring has shaped my professional life and whose seminal work in *Emotional Intelligence* has informed the substance of this book.

My thanks to Joann Daisen Mundth and Brent Jiku Derowitsch for sparking the ideas that conceived this book. And to Morgaine Sattva, Ruth Elaine Hane, and Laurie Young, my "dharma sisters," who held a vision for its highest good throughout these many months.

To Laura Friedman Williams, my agent, whose belief in this work, practical down-to-earth suggestions, and business acumen brought it to fruition. And to Molly Chehak, my editor at Warner Books, for her keen instincts, collaborative style, and consummate professionalism. Their assistance has been invaluable.

To my husband, Jim, whose steadfast love is more precious than a hundred thousand jewels. And with appreciation for the many friends and family in our community, including: Helen Stewart; Cathie and Ted Furman; Jason, Cindy, Grace, and Julia Jacobs; Ann-Marie and Randy Durushia; Linda Michel; Mary Froiland; Annie McKee; Scott Edelstein; and Natalie Goldberg. And to John, Kelly, Kari, and Andy Schultz; Carolyn and Shari Hess; Steve Schwandt; Gary Ukura; Mike Haldorson; and Erik Haugo for their help and support.

To the Clouds in Water sangha for their inspiration; and to the many whose stories appear, anonymously, in this text.

May any merit from this book be theirs.

CONTENTS

Introduction xiii

PART ONE: BREAKING TRAIL 1
Chapter 1. The Path 3
Chapter 2. The Science of Emotions 7

PART TWO: SELF 23
Chapter 3. Tuning In 25
  Taking Time to Breathe Mindfully 28
  Pausing in the Moment to Breathe 29
  Walking and Breathing 30
  Scanning Your Body for Tension Spots. . 35
Chapter 4: Naming Your Experience 41
  Doing a Daily Examen 47
  Sitting in Meditation 53
Chapter 5. Accepting What You Feel 59
  Reflecting on Your Emotional Habits. . . 63
  Welcoming Your Feelings Like an
   Old Friend 68
Chapter 6. Looking Deeply 72
  Investigating the Poisons of Your Mind . 76
  Asking Five Whys 82
  Seeing the Smoke in the Mirror 93
  Visualizing a Positive Model 96

Chapter 7. Staying Poised. 100
🏃 Creating a Circle of Protection 112
🏃 Visualizing Blue-Black Light to
    Counteract Anger 119
🏃 Imaging a Still Mountain 126

PART THREE: OTHER 133
Chapter 8. Deepening Empathy 135
🏃 Exchanging Yourself with Another. . . . 148
🏃 Breathing with One You Love 154
🏃 Doing Tong-Len: An Advanced
    Breathing Practice 156
Chapter 9. Living in Harmony 160
🏃 Picturing the Effects of Anger and Hatred . 172
🏃 Resolving Conflict 178
🏃 Asserting Limits with a Difficult Person 186
Chapter 10. Letting Go 197
🏃 Meditating with Equanimity Phrases. . . 206
Parting Words 211

Appendix 213
Notes. 217
For More Information 218

Wanderer, your footsteps are
the road, and nothing more;
wanderer, there is no road,
the road is made by walking.
By walking one makes the road,
and upon glancing behind
one sees the path . . .

ANTONIO MACHADO[1]

INTRODUCTION

The pace and complexity of modern life can over-
whelm even emotionally grounded people—affecting
our health, fraying our nerves, shaking our serenity. We
see our fleeting nature, moments passing like bubbles
in a stream, and ask anew, *What am I doing with my life?*
To attain the heights of joy and meaning, as well as the
solace of connection with our fellow wanderers, we face
a difficult climb. So we begin walking—unclear about
our direction, perhaps, unsure where to step. This path
to a deeper wisdom is an arduous but worthy journey, a
journey to which I hope this book acts as a guide and
companion.

Paths Are Made by Walking charts a course of travel that
integrates new knowledge about the brain with ancient
spiritual wisdom. It outlines a progression of easy-to-
access practices that lead to greater self-knowledge and
emotional intimacy in your relationships with others. As
a companion, it offers encouragement. But your footsteps are the road. Only upon glancing back will you see
the path.

Although the driving force of this book is practice,
the practice is grounded in recent scientific discovery.
As we grow, the brain develops complex and intricate
interconnections that form our personal and interpersonal habits. Modern brain imaging shows that meditative practice can help reshape the neural landscape,

making it fuller, richer, and healthier. With the right effort, we can etch new neuropathways in our brains. We can learn new ways for responding to life's pressures and stresses, joys and sorrows.

Because the time-honored wisdom contained in these pages changes us at our very core, it touches all areas of our lives. This book is for anyone who feels restless and unfocused, experiences pressure, clashes with coworkers, desires more intimacy with a partner, wants to be a better parent, or is looking for deeper wisdom. The hindrances that keep us from enjoying our personal lives and achieving professional success take many forms, from overload to emptiness to anger.

With the executives breathing down his neck, pressing for results, the latest assignment stretched this quiet, hard-working manager to his limits. As a team leader, he had to resolve both project-related problems and normal conflicts among members of the team. Data analysis he could handle. Problems with people were another matter.

After weeks of fifteen-hour days, crunching numbers, and "putting out fires" on a daily basis, he submitted a progress report. The boss—an ambitious man brought in to increase productivity and streamline operations—flagged him down in the hall "to ask him some questions" about the report. Furious about an error in the analysis, the boss, mincing no words, chewed him out right there in the hallway. It was brutal. His blood rose to his cheeks, skin burning with helpless humiliation. His mind went numb. He couldn't respond. "I just froze," he told me. "I was completely mortified." Normally a conscientious performer, he now goes to work with his stomach in knots, wishing he could quit.

•

Earlier in his life, he cared little for the fast track, but later on he became a successful sales executive. In a casual conversation, he confessed that his life satisfaction was at a "four or five on a scale of one to ten." For him to "rate" his life with a simple scale seemed out of character, not to mention the low marks. He used to be such a vibrant, curious guy; now he was bored with his job. The designer clothes and expensive cars somehow didn't provide happiness. When asked what he was doing for a spiritual practice these days, he deadpanned, "Making a lot of money."

•

On the drive home from a trying weekend with her parents, the kids in the backseat were arguing. Again. Mustering the last of her patience, she calmly asked them to keep it down but they didn't seem to hear. Louder, but still exercising momlike self-control, she threatened to take away TV privileges if they didn't stop . . . immediately! *The kids pointed fingers, blamed each other, and kept sniping in muffled tones until the car came to an abrupt halt on the side of the road. Snapping the gearshift into park, she yelled at the top of her voice that she couldn't—she* wouldn't *—stand another minute of this. Seeing their stricken faces, she turned back to the wheel, full of regret and ridden with guilt, and inched her way slowly back onto the road.*

As a consultant to individuals, couples, executives, performing artists, and professional athletes in the United States, Europe, and Asia, I've seen firsthand the desire for deeper, saner daily living. As a psychologist, I recognize the importance of modern science in lighting the path toward lasting change. And as a practitioner who has studied with spiritual directors from both West and East, I value the transforming power of meditative practice.

In my work, I am frequently asked why change is so hard and how to apply current research on the brain to bettering our daily lives. During a presentation for "high-potential leaders" in Los Angeles, a participant raised his hand. "Okay, okay," he said. "I get the point . . . but how can I *use* these ideas? Where is the 'guitar lesson'?" He was right, I thought. We don't expect a novice to pick up an instrument and just *know* how to play. We don't demand that an athlete perform complex skills without training. Why, then, should we expect people to develop emotional skills without regular practice? Just as the pathways in the brains of musicians and athletes have to be *formed*, we too need practice in order to make new connections in our emotional brains.

By integrating physiological, psychological, and spiritual knowledge, this book offers centuries-old applications for what modern science has now proved possible. Here you'll find an integrated approach, adapting Eastern practices within a framework provided by Western psychology. Although it incorporates spiritual methods, the book is a nonsectarian guide for walking a path toward greater equanimity, better emotional habits, and richer relationships. Conversion to a particular belief system is not necessary in order to benefit from the healing insights of the various traditions included. Toward this end, I have included practices from Eastern spirituality, the Christian contemplative tradition, and Western psychology.

You will learn about a hierarchy of capabilities that

build upon one another, beginning with a foundation of recognizing and regulating your emotions, then moving on to higher-level skills such as understanding and resolving conflicts. I have streamlined this process of personal development by first introducing a current model of the brain, then dividing the practices into two areas: working with Self and Other.

Starting with an overview in part 1, Breaking Trail, recent discoveries in neuroscience are discussed, shedding light on how our brain affects our reactions to the outside world—including the idea that our older, emotional brain can "override" our ability to think clearly if we are not aware. Understanding how the brain works provides a foundation for the hands-on practices that follow.

Part 2, Self, introduces fifteen practices for knowing our heart and managing our reactions. We begin by learning the basic, foundational practices that connect the mind and body. In subsequent chapters—Tuning In, Naming Your Experience, Accepting What You Feel, and Looking Deeply—we further our investigation of the sometimes elusive realms of the Self. Each of these areas cultivates deeper self-awareness, a valuable practice in and of itself. More important still, it is the basis for setting a new course in the world with others. Staying Poised completes the section on Self—addressing how we can use our newfound awareness to reshape our emotional habits. It offers strategies to stop us from going down the same old path the same old way.

The practices detailed in part 2 lay the foundation for better relationships with others. Part 3 presents seven additional practices. Deepening Empathy builds our capacity to "feel with" others, a core skill for more emotionally intimate and satisfying relationships at home and at work. These practices are drawn from the ancient Tibetan wisdom and Indian Tantric disciplines—offering ways to attune to the inner emotional tides of someone we seek to understand or connect with more deeply. We move from there to Living in Harmony, where the practices involve ways to resolve conflict with kind speech and upright action.

The final chapter, Letting Go, speaks to those circumstances in which we have done everything in our power to help. Despite our efforts, we can do nothing more. Here, I introduce the practice of Meditating with Equanimity Phrases. In times of extreme difficulty, we can hold these words close to restore emotional balance and to understand that we cannot control someone else's happiness or unhappiness. This practice works in concert with the profound wisdom of the Four Sublime Attitudes. Passed down over thousands of years, these attitudes are said to be the gateway to unshakable serenity.

The progression of practices follows an underlying framework based on research presented by my colleague and mentor Daniel Goleman in his seminal work *Emotional Intelligence*. Goleman offers scientific evidence about the brain's capacity to form new neural pathways. What I hope to add to his contribution is an understanding of *how* to bring about these changes. Meditative practice can reshape the brain and, consequently, affect our behaviors. This is a book about doing just that—blazing new trails in our neural pathways, in our understanding of self, and in our relationships with others.

There are many ways to use this book. You can treat it as a step-by-step guide, reading it through from cover to cover. You can write in the spaces provided, or keep a separate Personal Log to deepen your insight and strengthen your practice along the way. You can use it as a reference, turning to the sections and practices that speak to you in the moment, that rise to address what you face from day to day. Or you can leave it by your bedside, read it from time to time, and let it seep into your mind, shifting your consciousness in subtle ways.

But the book alone cannot find the path. It can only serve as a guide. Attaining inner peace is more than a peak experience or a moment captured. It is an ongoing journey, and your footsteps are the road to the serenity you seek.

PART ONE

BREAKING TRAIL

CHAPTER 1

THE PATH

All paths lead to the same goal: to convey to others what we are. And we must pass through solitude and difficulty, isolation and silence, in order to reach forth to the enchanted place where we can dance our clumsy dance and sing our sorrowful song—but in this dance or in this song there are fulfilled the most ancient rites of our conscience in the awareness of being human and of believing in a common destiny.

PABLO NERUDA[1]

SIKKIM PROVINCE, INDIA. 1995. We began our Himalayan trek as strangers with a common goal: six Americans decked out in jewel-toned Gore-Tex, Polarfleece, and state-of-the-art hiking boots; a team of yaks bearing tents, ropes, gear, and wicker-caged chickens; three Sherpa cooks balancing baskets of potatoes, turnips, pots, and pans atop their heads; all climbing to the spectacular western rim of Kanchenjunga peak. A Sikkimese guide led the way, wearing tennis shoes, thin cotton pants, a lightweight jacket, and a rag bandanna.

By the fifth day, two Americans had succumbed to altitude sickness, one carried back to the village on a yak, the other leaning on the shoulder of a Sherpa who volunteered to go back down. The rest of us continued up the mountain, cutting through fog and mist and haze to a clearing at eleven thousand feet. We made camp by a lake near a rock-pile shrine to the "weather gods" and ate lentils and fry bread. Only the braying of yaks, the flapping of prayer flags, and the occasional, distant call of a hawk broke the silence. To keep warm in the cold moist air, we put hot-water bottles in our bedclothes and went to sleep beneath a low, heavy sky.

At morning's first light, a Sherpa tapped on the tent. "Madam. Wake now. Snow. Big snow." Peeking out, I saw the ground covered in a thick white blanket. Clouds concealed our destination: the summit of Kanchen-junga. It would be a difficult day for trekking.

After hurrying through a breakfast of fried egg sandwiches smothered in hot pepper sauce, chai, and the daily dose of garlic soup to prevent altitude sickness, we started off—snow still falling, fresh water and chocolate bars in our packs. The Sherpa cooks and yaks had gone ahead, but when we left an hour later, the trail was blocked, buried beneath the blowing drifts. We set out in another direction, stumbling, unable to catch a full breath in the thinning air.

The new route led us into a deep, ice-encrusted valley. Without a clear path to follow, we shared the grueling task of breaking our own. Even the strongest among us grew exhausted after only ten or fifteen minutes in the lead. We distracted ourselves with small talk about movies and the warm comforts of home. Now and then the guide would pause, adjust his rag bandanna, and squint into the unforgiving glare. Gradually, his air of authority became a look of uncertainty. We were lost.

Talk of movies ceased, leaving only the silence of falling snow, the squeak of boots, and a strained chorus of breathing. "Too far east," said the guide, pointing. From that moment on we kept a code of silence, fearing that even the whisper of a complaint would crack our will to continue. Forced to change our direction again, we had to cross into more unfamiliar territory, break more trail.

Slight in frame and older than the others, I struggled to lead for even five minutes. Numbed with cold sweat and melted snow, I found just keeping up at the back of the group difficult. In order to forge ahead, mental focus narrowed to the simple act of taking the next step. Muscles quivering, I used my arms to hoist my legs up and over the surface of the snow before they crunched back down through the crust for another step forward. Up and over. One more time. And again.

We plodded on, sharing water and rationing chocolate, glancing back at our tracks—our record of progress. As we caught sight of our rendezvous point, whoops and hollers of exhausted joy broke the grim silence. As we made our way to the trekkers' shed, disheveled and shivering, the Sherpa cooks grinned, clapped, and raised their arms in welcome . . . and relief. We took long breaths of garlic soup and smoke from the cooking fire—civilization at last. Inside, we peeled off wet layers, huddled by the fire, and drank hot tea with sweet milk. Strangers no longer.

Upon my return from India, I resumed my consulting work throughout the United States. Listening to people talk about pressure on the job and conflict with loved ones, I reflected on my own struggle during the trek in Sikkim. The difficulty of changing our lives for the better is very much like the effort required for each step on that path to Kanchenjunga.

When confronted with the gathering storms, high winds, and deep snow of our emotional minds, we must make a parallel effort to etch new pathways in the brain. Like creating new trails on the way to the summit, we can, through mindful practice, change our behavior—passing through the undiscovered terrain of self to the warm shed of better relationships and shared experience.

As we prepare for this journey, it may help to first look at the map, get a feel for the territory, and examine in greater detail the topographic features of the emotional brain. A closer look will familiarize us with the well-worn neural trails that make up our emotional habits. Though our existing habits often get us to our destination, we may miss some of the emotional richness—the more sublime scenery and hidden beauty—found in new behaviors and reactions.

And then there are times when our habits lead us entirely in the wrong direction. We get lost or hurt, or do damage to our relationships. To determine the most rewarding route, it helps to understand how and why our habits and reactions are so strong—and not always in keeping with our intentions. To get a closer look at why this is so, we turn now to "the brain" inset on the map of self-discovery.

CHAPTER 2

THE SCIENCE OF EMOTIONS

The signals of the world are different now, the dangers greater, and our old system of unconscious adaptation has reached its limits. We haven't needed to direct our minds consciously all that much until now, and we haven't really understood the delicacy and absolute necessity of doing so—until now.

ROBERT ORNSTEIN[1]

The operating system of our emotional mind—the limbic system—contains a small neural cluster, the *amygdala* (pronounced ah-*mig*-dah-lah), designed to react quickly, an ever-vigilant security system keeping us safe from harm. It is an older part of the brain, and has served us well for centuries.

But the world we now face has changed. In the past, conflict was often a life-or-death matter. Today the threats—different from those faced by our ancestors—are more often symbolic than real. They are the modern equivalent of "eat or be eaten" and often involve conflicts in the work environment, which may seem to threaten an individual's dignity, livelihood, or pride. Just as modern computer technology is built upon the designs and operating systems of the past, the thinking brain—or neocortex—evolved from the limbic system. Despite this advance, a glitch remains. Unlike the computer, where the old is quickly surpassed by the new, our ancient brain is actually *faster* than the thinking brain, and can override our more reasoned desires. The amygdala was designed to react to *any* threat as a life-or-death situation—a good thing if we are physically confronted in a dark parking lot, but not so helpful in a symbolic conflict with a coworker or family member.

It works like this: When the brain receives stimuli, the amygdala scans all prior emotional experience, looking for a match. If it recognizes a frightening, humiliating, or threatening experience, the amygdala activates our ancient survival instincts: "fight back," or "run for your life." Because the neurocircuitry of the limbic system is old and less than precise, it is not always able to distinguish a symbolic threat from genuine physical danger. Sometimes it signals a false alarm. The highly tuned amygdala might misread an unusual sound at night as a burglar when it's really just the wind in the bushes.

Our thinking brain *can* distinguish a real threat from a symbolic one, but sometimes it takes too long to "download" its rational assessment. The amygdala's reaction comes instantly, engulfing us in a knee-jerk, fight-or-flight reaction. Daniel Goleman, in *Emotional Intelligence,* calls this either an "amygdala hijacking" or an "emotional hijacking." I prefer the term *amygdala hijacking.* The following chart will help you recognize its telltale signs:

SIGNS OF AN AMYGDALA HIJACKING[2]

Daniel Goleman, in *Emotional Intelligence,* describes the following four hallmarks of an amygdala hijack. They are the litmus test for whether you have been emotionally hijacked.

- First, there is usually a triggering event: someone's nasty tone of voice, a confrontation with a coworker, an "attitude" held by a loved one, a clash in cultural values, an incident of mistreatment, or a situation that threatens something dear to us.

- Second, we experience an instant physical reaction: Our heart pounds, our palms get sweaty, a knot closes our throat, our knees feel weak, or our mind goes blank. This physical arousal happens due to the burst of stress hormones signaled by the amygdala and released in the body.

- Hand in hand, we feel strong emotions of anger, fear, or numbness. We see red, become irate, freeze in fear, are swallowed in embarrassment, cringe in shame, or feel nothing at all.

- Last, we react: automatically, in nanoseconds, without thinking. Either we explode—honk furiously, tell someone off, snap, make a cutting comment—or we implode, hold our frustration, lose concentration, bite our tongue, grind our teeth, worry late at night, or criticize ourselves without mercy.

In the throes of an amygdala hijack, we react with our most primitive, least conscious instincts. Our neural impulses travel down the most well-used pathway in the brain—the trail of our most ingrained emotional habits. If we are accustomed to shouting when angry, that reaction is likely to be triggered; if we tend to "stuff" and "never let them see us sweat," we may implode. If we see the worst case and believe in doom, chances are we will get depressed.

At the point of a full amygdala hijacking, our emotions are so intense, and our perspective so clouded, that there is little hope of understanding another viewpoint or acting in a reasonable way.

The fact that we experience amygdala hijacks *does not* indicate a personal weakness or character flaw; the brain is simply doing what it was designed to do. Knowing this helps us anticipate and prepare for our brain's automatic reactions. If we can't change the underlying architecture of our brains, we *can* adjust its programming. Once we understand how the brain works, we can short-circuit our involuntary reactions and reshape neural pathways to better suit the symbolic threats of today's world. We can reconfigure our default response by creating new neural connections—making the healthy pathways more heavily traveled and easier to follow.

Now let's look at some examples of amygdala hijacks in our lives.

Even though it's hectic during the holiday season, she always worked hard to make Christmas a perfect day: last-minute shopping, wrapping gifts, baking, and preparing traditional Swedish meatballs and lefse *for dinner. After rushing around all day, she lit the candles and called to her family, steam rising from the carefully prepared food. Then everyone showed up at the table—late. Her fifteen-year-old daughter didn't have her "hair done." Her son didn't hear the call for dinner over his Walkman. Her husband was "finishing something" at his workbench. By the time they finally arrived, the steam had stopped rising from the food. She glared at them in cold silence. Dinner was tense with the scraping of silverware on china. When it came to opening presents, she sat in a chair, read the newspaper, and didn't say a word the rest of the evening.*

•

Just the sounds of the office assistant's voice aggravated her instantly—that, and long lunches, late arrivals, and

Web surfing during work hours. Talking to the boss got her nowhere. She couldn't take it anymore—she'd had enough of his "slacker ways." Opening her file drawer, she took out an armful of thick files.

"I couldn't help myself," she told me. "I knew the assistant hated copying. He felt it was beneath him. So I went to his cube and 'apologetically' asked him to make photocopies of the files for an 'urgent' report due at the end of the day. 'Top priority,' I said. 'The veep asked for it directly. Have it done before you leave today.'" Each time the assistant brought back copies, she thanked him, handed him another pile, shut the office door, and fed the copies of the phantom report into the shredder.

•

A young teacher wanted to make a good impression, so he volunteered for extra duties to show his school spirit, helping out with clubs and other activities in addition to his regular class load. It was exhilarating at first, but after a while, just keeping up with grading and preparing lessons demanded more time than he had. At the end of the quarter, with grades due the next morning, he sat alone at his desk. The sky was dark. Everyone else had gone home hours ago. Faced with a stack of unmarked essays, unfinished grades, and the next day's lesson plans, his mind jammed, unable to focus on what to do next. Paralyzed, he stared at the empty desks in his classroom.

Amygdala hijackings take many forms, sabotaging our lives and work. The good news is we *can*, with greater self-awareness, rewire our brains for a more effective response to the stresses that trigger them.

HOW HABITS FORM

Although we don't like to think of ourselves as living our lives on autopilot, the truth is that habits govern much of what we do. Anything we learn and everything we do results from neurons firing and connecting, forming and re-forming pathways. Habits are simply pathways that get used a lot—many of them for very good reasons.

Take the basic but important matter of where your keys are right now. Chances are you know their exact location, even though you don't remember how they got there. At some point in the past, you made a decision about where your keys go when you aren't using them to open the door or start the car. Once, you had to think about it. That thought was a chain of neurons firing. Each time you set your keys on the dresser at the end of the day, those linked neurons became a well-developed pathway—so well groomed, so efficient, that where you put your keys now requires no conscious effort. Because you are in the habit of setting them in a certain place—on the dresser, on a hook by the door, or in the zipper pocket of your purse—they will be right where they always are.

If, at the end of each day, you were in the habit of letting your keys fall where they may, you would have to search for them every morning. Each day would start with checking your pockets or rummaging through your handbag in a harried search. Developing a habit of putting your keys in the same place each time you come home makes your life easier.

Other habits—like chewing fingernails—do little to assist daily living. They may begin as an innocuous response to tension. We get nervous, we chew on a fingernail, and a pathway for fingernail chewing develops. The more frequently we chew our nails, the thicker the neural pathway becomes, forming a more efficient neural highway for chewing our nails. Over time, these pathways continue to strengthen and eventually become like a wide, fast neural interstate. This well-traveled freeway shapes our "default" response, and we chew our nails without realizing it. Despite our resolve to stop, a habit has formed and we are now hiding our unsightly nails in embarrassment.

If you are a nail biter, you know that it does little to alleviate stress and in fact creates more anxiety. Now you may be concerned about hiding your nails and wondering if others see you as nervous and worried. To remedy any adverse habit, you first must stop doing what "you have always done," and then replace it with a more helpful alternative. Maybe you decide that when you are nervous, from now on you will just fold your hands instead of biting your nails. During the transition period, you may still find yourself occasionally biting your nails, but given time a stronger neural pathway will develop. The new, better habit will replace the old.

EMOTIONAL HABITS

Where we put our keys and how we respond to nervousness are somewhat harmless examples, but they illustrate the way habits are formed and the difficulties involved with changing them. Emotional habits follow the same rules, but their complexity presents a greater challenge for change. Stemming from the amygdala-controlled response, our emotional reactions form pathways that strengthen with each repetition of thought,

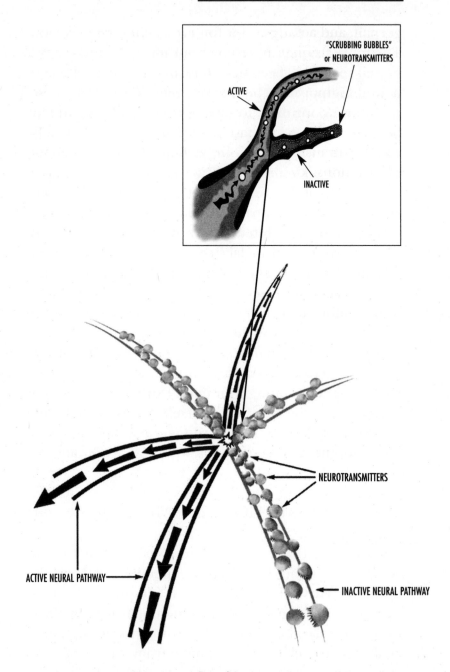

Figure 2.1
The bubbles here represent neurotransmitters washing away unused neural pathways.

feeling, and action. When confronted with a similar situation, the stronger network of neurons prevails.

Just as with the more benign habits, we need a two-pronged approach in order to reshape an emotional habit: First, we extinguish the old habit. With disuse, the old neural connections (old habits) are cleaned up by neurotransmitters, which wash away unused synaptic connections, kind of like scrubbing bubbles.[3]

Second, we need to develop a new habit in its place. As we continue to use the new strategy, it becomes the preferred neural pathway. If we do this repeatedly, the new connections become stronger than the old: "When a habit is dysfunctional, replacing it with a more effective one requires enough practice of the better habit— and inhibition of the poor one—that the neural circuitry for the old behavior finally withers . . . and the circuitry for the better behavior grows stronger."[4]

This is no small task. Once established, deeply ingrained neural connections are hard to retread. During an amygdala hijack—and especially when we are stressed or tired—we regress to our most automatic, least sophisticated reactions, such as yelling when angry, panicking when lost, or pouting when we don't get our way. Until new pathways are created with the conscious effort and repetition of a new behavior, our older pathways will win out.

SLOW DOWN: NEURAL HIGHWAYS UNDER CONSTRUCTION

Our struggle to change emotional habits stems from the brain's design. Joseph LeDoux, in *The Emotional Brain*, illustrates the problem: ". . . the wiring of the

The dark arrows represent neuropathways traveling *from* the amygdala *to* the thinking brain. The brain's design provides greater access for these pathways than the white ones, traveling back toward the amygdala.

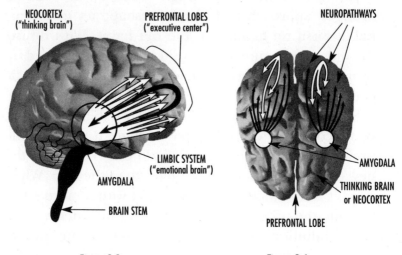

Figure 2.3
Side view of the brain.

Figure 2.4
Top view of the brain.

brain at this point in our evolutionary history is such that connections from the emotional systems to the cognitive systems are stronger than connections from the cognitive systems to the emotional systems."[5] Like traffic control in many major cities, where more lanes are open going one way during rush hour, the brain's design provides greater access *from* the amygdala *to* the thinking brain. On the other hand, fewer lanes go in the opposite direction. A message from the executive center to the amygdala can get caught up like a commuter in a traffic jam.

But relief from this congestion can be found in another feature of brain function. We know that "the basic design of the brain is built around a simple opposition: Some neurons initiate action, and others inhibit the same action."[6] The first step is to recognize we are engaged in our habitual response and then *pause*, interrupting the impulses of firing neurons from shooting down their well-worn paths. To do this, we need help, and help comes from the decision-making center of the brain: the prefrontal lobes. By increasing the ability of the left prefrontal lobe to inhibit the action of the amygdala, we improve and expand the ability of our thinking brain to better control adverse reactions.

When we resist our "knee-jerk" responses—our oldest, most deeply formed habits—and repeat the practice of a new response *(Deep breath . . . stay cool),* our brain creates new neuropathways. We are opening up new channels of communication, additional "traffic lanes" *from* the thinking brain *to* the emotional brain. More inhibitory neurons can fire to override the primal reactions of the amygdala and shut down its response. The "inhibitory circuit between the prefrontal lobes and the amygdala underlies . . . our ability to stay calm in the face of stress, crisis, uncertainty, and shifting challenges. The prefrontal lobes' ability to inhibit the amygdala's message preserves mental clarity and keeps our actions on a steady course."[7]

RESHAPING OUR NEUROPATHWAYS

We are in constant search of new ways to help us overcome anxiety, guilt, shame, and similarly disruptive emotions. Current remedies include the use of prescription drugs (and controlled substances) at a level unprecedented in human history. Western research has focused most of its energy on developing more efficient drugs, with some success. Though drugs can help to alleviate many problems—and in some cases, even cure ailments—they are not the only answer. There is an old alternative: meditative practice.

Advances in the study of the brain offer new evidence supporting the benefits of these ancient strategies. Even though it is difficult to document precisely what changes the brain undergoes during meditation, test subjects experience improvement in brain function.

Richard Davidson, researcher and director of the Laboratory for Affective Neuroscience, conducted a breakthrough study with employees at Promega, a biotech company in Madison, Wisconsin. A group of scientists gathered daily for eight weeks to practice mindfulness meditation—sitting and contemplating their breath in total awareness of the present moment. At the conclusion of the study, the participants reported feeling calmer, more focused, and more creative.

More impressive still, researchers documented "positive changes in the scientists' *brain function* as a direct result of the . . . training," and the results showed that the subjects' ". . . left prefrontal lobes—the brain area that suppresses amygdala hijacks and generates positive feelings—[became] significantly more active."[8] In the Promega study, the prefrontal lobe's increased activity strengthened and enhanced its inhibitory role. In other words, this "sense of greater alertness is no mere illusion: It stems from an underlying change in the brain." Furthermore, "this brain change duplicates that found in those individuals who are most resilient and adaptable under stress. The finding suggests that as a competence such as self-control strengthens, so do the corresponding circuits in the brain."[9]

After reading about these experiments in meditation, I was intrigued, but not surprised at the results. What I found truly remarkable, though, was that the scientists didn't just "feel better." Their brains had physically *changed*, reinforcing my belief in the rewards of meditative practice.

But simply marveling at the breakthroughs in brain research cannot alter the course of our lives. It is one thing to pursue awareness with theory and research, quite another to put it into practice. In fact, for complex emotional habits, the practice period of maximal effect may be *at least six months to two years*. The following chart provides more information on the process of changing our emotional habits.

STAGES OF CHANGING AN EMOTIONAL HABIT

Here is a brief outline of the stages we go through when reshaping an emotional habit. Perhaps you will recognize some of the places you have already been. You may also get a glimpse of where you are going.

Stage 1: Awakening a Desire to Change
Before starting this journey, we probably didn't pay much attention to the frequency of our feelings or the density of our thoughts. In the initial stage, awareness dawns—we begin to see behavioral patterns, recognizing a need for change and kindling a desire for a better way to respond.

Stage 2: Deepening Self-Awareness
Next, we grow in our self-awareness—at both a perceptual and a neural level. It may seem as if our thoughts have increased in quantity, that our mind is utterly congested, our emotions rampant (the "conscious incompetence" phase of developing new skills). This stage can be discouraging, as if we are getting worse before getting better.

In fact, our discordant thoughts and feelings have not increased in quantity; rather, we are more aware at deeper levels. Becoming aware (activating the prefrontal cortex) is a necessary and crucial step toward changing habits that are negative or undesirable.

Stage 3: Seeing Patches of Change for the Better

By this time, we can maintain change for the better, but in short spurts. Relapses to the old are frequent and recurrent, but there is a *trend* toward the new. Reaching the point where a new habit replaces the old takes extensive practice—studies of behavior change find that the longer people work at changing, the more durable the change will be. Weeks are better than days; months are better than weeks.

Stage 4: Fine-Tuning

Now we see more subtle levels to our habits and patterns. "Skeletons" hiding in our closet are likely to come out. We may look back at opportunities passed by, or things we have done with regret, remorse, or self-criticism. In this stage, we can recognize and work with very subtle parts of our emotional life—averting destructive thoughts, overreactions, or old behaviors early on, as they appear.

Stage 5: Having a New Default Behavior

In the final stages, the new habit becomes our default response (even when we are pressured and stressed), indicating that a new neuropathway is deeply etched in the brain. At this point, our new way of acting or reacting has stabilized, making a relapse to the old habit unlikely. We have arrived in a state of greater self-control and equipoise!

We know change is possible in our neuropathways and in our everyday lives. But how do we do it? How do we retool ourselves for lasting transformation?

An answer can be found in the Sutra on the Establishments of Mindfulness,[10] a blueprint for mindfulness that has been studied, practiced, and handed down with special care from generation to generation for twenty-five hundred years. Broadening the "Know Thyself" maxim of the West, these ancient Eastern teachings provide instructions for developing mindful awareness: tuning in, naming and accepting our emotions, and then investigating the root causes of our struggles.

The Sutra text[11] teaches us to become mindful by observing the body *in* the body; the feelings *in* the feelings; and the mind *in* the mind. This involves the paradox of observing from the inside out *and* the outside in. The Establishments of Mindfulness instruct us to progress from first being conscious of our physical selves, noticing the signs of stress and tension carried in the body. Next, we move to observing the emotional self, learning to name what we feel without criticism. Once we've touched our feelings, we then study our mind, noticing how our thought patterns skew our view of the world.

The thought of developing mindfulness in our busy and demanding world may seem foreign, even cumbersome, at first. But the rewards are worth the effort. Over the centuries and across cultural lines, this blueprint for self-awareness has opened the heart of human consciousness. If we want better relationships, less fear of conflict, more skill in resolving differences, improved leadership qualities, greater certainty in decision making, or better responses to daily stresses, we need *more* than the force of the analytical mind. It takes doing. One step. Up and over. And again.

TRAILHEAD

Here you are poised to take the first step, gathering energy to embark on a practical, spiritual journey toward a deeper understanding of your self, your life, and your relationships. Your course—charted for centuries by religious teachers, philosophers, sages, saints, and scientists—will be an exploration of previously unknown personal territory, opening you to an extraordinary potential for transforming your life. This road leads, ultimately, to greater understanding and harmony with others.

Finding the way necessitates breaking new trails in the brain, etching better habits of mind and new patterns of connections. And in order to "reach forth to the enchanted place," you must go through yourself, into the solitude of self-discovery, the silence of seeing what you are, the sting of admitting that your actions may have been a "clumsy dance." It is, at times, a difficult and even lonely task, requiring honesty and determination. But new responses *are* possible. You *can* retool the pathways of your brain. You *can* mold and reshape the very structure of your emotional habits. Take a breath. And begin.

PART TWO

SELF

CHAPTER 3

TUNING IN

You don't need to leave your room. Remain sitting at your table and listen. Don't even listen, simply wait. Don't even wait. Be quite still and solitary. The world will freely offer itself to you. To be unmasked, it has no choice.

FRANZ KAFKA[1]

We begin cultivating the ancient practice of mindfulness by taking time to slow down from the hectic pace of work and life. Breathe deeply and pay attention. Here. Now.

Tuning in means pausing long enough to recognize rising tension, stirring emotions and the acts they prompt—the real-time scenes of our lives. "Just as a film editor runs a film in slow motion, frame by frame . . . so we have to slow down our lives if we want to make adjustments or improvements to the overall picture."[2]

But slowing down in the rush and hustle of our tightly scheduled lives is easier said than done. There are times—more often than I care to admit—when the query "How are you?" is too difficult to answer. I haven't asked myself. I don't know.

A feverish pace is endemic to the Western world: too much to do, no time to ponder, priorities lost, perspective blurred, resiliency drained. We feel a sense of

urgency and pull in, close our perspective, develop a
kind of emotional myopia. Problems are put on hold.
We can deal with them . . . later. *Faster, faster* is the
mantra of our age, making us vulnerable to amygdala
hijacks. Nerves get frayed. We've had enough. *Snap.*

The telltale sign of an amygdala hijack is a rush of
strong emotion: anger, fear, or numbness. Anger is the
most obvious. Intense emotion often clouds our perspective, and we are incapable of measured thought or
reasonable action. This may show itself in fits of uncon-
trolled behavior—we shred papers to get even, lash out
in rage, put up a cold wall with loved ones, or stop
speaking to colleagues at work.

But an amygdala hijack does not always result in
anger. Sometimes these hijack moments play out differently, causing us to shut down or get anxious when
stress builds up. We find ourselves feeling numb, for-
getting appointments, retreating from conflict, or
staying locked in a job—too paralyzed to move. Once
the amygdala takes over, our instinctive, least sophisticated habits—the most well-traveled pathways in the
brain—take control. The automatic reaction, whatever
its emotional tone, beats our rational response to the
punch.

Just as earthquakes measure differently on a Richter
scale, amygdala hijackings fluctuate from low-grade
simmering and worrying to full-blown yelling and over-
reacting. More often than not, our stress is alleviated
before any serious problems occur, and we return to
our normal selves. Sometimes, however, the angry outbursts, obsessive worrying, or pent-up silence of an
amygdala hijack damages our relationships or impairs
our performance at work.

Without seeking deeper awareness, we risk living in

default mode, where the unsophisticated, unconscious, and automatic reactions to pressure-filled days shape our emotional lives. Even though we know better, the emotional brain takes over. We don't really *want* to fight, get angry, or be impatient, but we do.

Mindfulness is the key to countering an amygdala hijack—developing an "observing self," looking more deeply for the root of what triggers our reactions. The essence of mindfulness is universal. At its core lies the simple act of paying attention to our most basic life function: *breathing*.

Inhaling. Exhaling. Breathing in. Breathing out. Nothing more.

Everything we need for developing self-awareness is right at our fingertips if we tune in and make awareness a part of daily life. "The way of awareness is always here, always accessible to you, in each moment. . . ."[3]

TUNING IN TO THE BREATH

"Being with the breath" is the heart of Eastern meditation, the foundation for all other practices. It is the hours spent learning to walk before dancing, the first chords on the guitar. Paying attention to the breath returns us to our beginnings and marks the starting point for cultivating awareness. Even after lifetimes of developing mindfulness skills, practitioners still return to the basics of breathing.

I learned this version of focused breathing in my studies with Thich Nhat Hanh, a soft-spoken monk, scholar, poet, and peace activist who teaches this simple practice at Plum Village, his monastery in southern France.

In this practice, we use the breath to become aware of what *is*—in the moment. Following the road map provided by the Sutra on the Establishments of Mindfulness, we begin by turning our attention to the subtle language of the body. Noticing the rhythms of our breathing, the strength or faintness of our pulse, the rising and falling of our emotions. "When you are hungry, you breathe in a special way; when you're full, you breathe in a special way; when you're happy, you breathe in a special way. . . ."[4] The body, beginning with the essence of the breath, portrays our state of mind and being.

Breathing mindfully, we become aware of what *is*. Right here. Right now.

PRACTICES

TAKING TIME TO BREATHE MINDFULLY

This practice asks you to set a specific time in your day to be with yourself and notice what you are experiencing *in the moment.*

WHAT YOU'LL NEED

- About ten to fifteen minutes of uninterrupted time.

- A quiet, private place to be still and reflect.

TRY THIS

- Begin by straightening your back while sitting, standing, or lying down. Assume a comfortable but alert position. Allow your breath to flow easily.

- Focus on your breathing. Feel it come in and go out, in and out. Keep full awareness on the in-breath, full awareness on the out-breath. Let the breath just happen, observing it wherever and however you feel it—a rise and fall of your belly, a coolness in your nose, a pressure in your lungs ... simply ride the waves of your own breath.

- As you breathe in, say to yourself, *Breathing in, I know I am breathing in.* And as you breathe out, say, *Breathing out, I know I am breathing out.* Recognize your in-breath as an in-breath and your out-breath as an out-breath. Then shorten your words, saying only, *In, Out. In, Out.*

- If you become distracted, you can put your hand on your knees or your belly, close your eyes, or adjust your posture to a more stable position, bringing your attention back to breathing.

- When your mind wanders, notice what pulled your attention away, then let it go, returning to the in and out sensations of your breath.

- Try breathing in this way once a day for at least a week. Begin with five minutes, and then gradually increase your breathing time to ten minutes or more.

PAUSING IN THE MOMENT TO BREATHE

This practice asks that you pause briefly during your day (in the car, in the shower, during a break or routine task at work), and ...

TRY THIS

- Take a moment to tune in by listening to the rhythm of your breathing.

- Become aware of your thoughts and feelings in these moments, just allowing them to pass as if you are watching a parade. Resist the habit of judging yourself or what you see. Simply notice what *is*.

- After you've paused to breathe mindfully, make a mental note of anything that might have changed in you as a result. What did you notice by pausing to breathe mindfully? What physical or emotional sensations did you experience? How did your perspective shift, even momentarily?

WALKING AND BREATHING

An alternative way of bringing awareness into your life is walking and breathing. If you are an active person who finds sitting difficult, this variation may be useful for you. Here we just walk, bringing our awareness to the experience of walking itself, not trying to get anywhere in particular. Without thinking, hurrying, or planning ahead, we walk and breathe.

TRY THIS

- Begin walking and breathing at a slower-than-normal pace.

- Bring your attention to the sensations in your feet or legs, feeling your body in motion. Notice your foot contacting the ground. Feel your weight shift as the other foot lifts and moves forward, coming down to make contact with the ground in turn. Again. With each step.

- Bring awareness of your breathing into each step, breathing in as your foot lifts up, breathing out as it meets the ground. Do this with each step you take, walking at any pace. Although some people like to practice walking meditation at a slow pace, the idea is to be *aware* at *whatever pace* you are moving.

- To deepen your concentration, keep your gaze focused out in front of you while you walk, rather than looking at your feet or taking in the scenery. Just be with each step, realizing that you are just where you are, in each moment, noticing the sensations in your feet.

- If your mind wanders, or if you feel self-conscious, gently bring your attention back to the movement of your feet, legs, and body.

- Try walking and breathing for at least five minutes, then gradually increase your walking periods to ten minutes or more. After you've completed a period of walking and breathing, take a moment to make a mental note of any changes in mood you experienced as a result.

If you are particularly agitated, angry, or bereaved, it may be beneficial to do walking and breathing. There are those moments or days when we can hardly stand to be in our own skin. We need to move, get something out of our system. At these times, walking and breathing may be the best—and perhaps the *only*—awareness practice we can do.

TUNING IN TO THE BODY

After four or five hits on the snooze alarm, an ambitious young marketing consultant with a major national firm often started her day with a Diet Coke and a couple of cigarettes. She'd had five straight nights of insomnia before the last "make it or break it" presentation for a big account . . . and then the dizzy spells began. She suffered from irritability, exhaustion, loneliness, and poor concentration. Then the minor annoyances and ringing in her ears turned into months of depression; just getting out of bed was her greatest challenge. "Why didn't I pay attention? Why didn't anyone else notice?" she asked me.

Paying attention to the body is a vital source of knowledge, an internal monitor that alerts us to deeper emotional states . . . if we pay attention. But too often we are distracted, caught by surprise when our body "speaks up"—head throbbing, back aching, or jaw clenched. When we aren't tuned in, we can miss the connection between our rat-race pace and our physical symptoms. Maybe we have been ignoring the physical toll of a negative environment at home or at work. Perhaps we are exhausted, burdened, and don't know why.

The practice of scanning for tension spots activates the thinking brain and engages our mind–body connection. But really paying attention to the body's signals requires adopting a "beginner's mind," as if we were seeing for the first time. The following story, passed on from the time of Gautama Buddha in the sixth century B.C.E., describes the open and observant mind-set necessary for this practice:[5]

> A group of monks gathered after a long day of begging for alms, legs aching and feet blistered from the miles traveled in straw sandals. They sat, after a meager meal of cooked rice and wilted greens, sipping jasmine tea and talking about the meaning of life. They were in heated discussion, debating how to practice "mindfulness of the body," wondering about the "great fruit and great benefit" promised by the teachings on this subject.
>
> Gautama, who had just come down from the meditation hall for a cup of tea, interrupted them, saying, "What's all the commotion? This must be something good. What are you monks talking about?"
>
> Startled, they answered, "We were talking about the proper way to 'feel the body in the body.' Can you tell us how to develop and cultivate this practice so that it is of great fruit and great benefit?"
>
> Gautama sat down, pausing to look over the dining hall, monks finishing dishes in the nearby kitchen, and instructed his students in this way:
>
> "Imagine a sack which can be opened at both ends, containing a variety of grains—brown rice, wild rice, mung beans, kidney beans, sesame seeds, white rice. When someone with good eyesight opens the bag, he will review it like this: 'This is brown rice, this is wild rice, these are mung beans, these are kidney beans, these are sesame seeds, this is white rice.' Just so, the practitioner passes in review the whole of his body from the soles of his feet to the hair on the top of the head. . . ."[6]

Scanning the body with curiosity and without judgment—as more than just a plain old sack of beans—requires "good eyesight," keen attention to the nuances of stress. Increasing sensitivity to your body's early warning signs by noticing the hot spots that carry tension and store emotions can reduce the length and intensity of an amygdala hijack, short-circuiting the consequences.

Say you suffer from chronic headaches. During a body scan, you notice something more subtle—that your teeth are also often sore. Later you realize that on the days you get headaches, your teeth hurt when you wake up. Then, on the morning of an important meeting, your teeth are especially sore. You realize you have been grinding them in the night. Aha! Worrying causes you to grind your teeth; then you get a headache. By scanning your body, you uncover the root cause of a much more general pain—worrying without being aware.

Some Common Early Warning Signs

Your heart starts to pound; your temples are tight; you have butterflies in your stomach; there is pain in your chest; your shoulders get tight; you feel a headache coming on.

More Signs

The muscles in your neck are rigid; upsetting pictures flash through your mind; there are knots between your shoulder blades; your face flushes; your jaw locks; tears well up in your eyes; you have trouble breathing; you find it hard to focus on anything; your forehead or palms sweat.

AND MORE

You get a "pins-and-needles" or tingling feeling; you lose your train of thought; you become lightheaded or dizzy; your mouth is dry; you start trembling; your hands get cold.

The body tension scan helps move us from tangible, physical signs of tension to deeper levels of awareness, making us less vulnerable to amygdala hijacks. Becoming more deeply aware counteracts our tendency to live unconsciously and miss the variety and richness of our inner life.

PRACTICE

SCANNING YOUR BODY FOR TENSION SPOTS

This practice asks you to make time: Shut the bedroom door, turn off the TV, or wake up early. Tune in to your body. Listen to what it is saying. At the University of Massachusetts Medical Center's Clinic for Stress Reduction and Relaxation—founded by researcher and Zen practitioner Jon Kabat-Zinn—the body tension scan has demonstrated remarkable results with cardiac, cancer, and hypertension patients. For patients with life-threatening illnesses, the scan is a forty-five-minute practice, but you may adjust it to the demands of your life. A good starting goal is about ten minutes.

WHAT YOU'LL NEED

- About ten to fifteen minutes of uninterrupted time.

- A quiet, private place to relax.

- A notebook, blank book, or journal, from now on called your Personal Log. (*Note:* Future practices will, at times, ask you to reflect and write in your Personal Log. Keeping your responses together in such a log helps you track progress, reveals patterns in your emotional habits, and provides a snapshot of your work in developing greater emotional intelligence.)

TRY THIS

- Lie on your back or sit comfortably in a chair. Take a few moments to breathe. Feel your breath coming in and going out. Be aware of each in-breath and out-breath.

- After about two or three minutes, move your mind through the different regions of your body, lingering in each region, breathing *through* each region, slowly, paying attention to what you find there.

- If you don't feel anything in a certain area of your body, then "not feeling anything" is your experience in that moment. Simply make a mental note of it and move on.

- Start with the toes of your left foot and slowly move up the foot and leg to the pelvic region, feeling the sensations as you go, directing the breath to the area. From there, go down to the toes of your right foot, then back up the right leg to your pelvis.

- Now move up through the torso, lower back, and abdomen, then through the upper back and chest to the shoulders. If your mind wanders, as it naturally will, gently bring it back to the part of the body you were working with when it began to drift.

- Go next to the fingers of both hands and simultaneously move up both arms, along with your back, to the shoulders. Now move through the neck and throat. Finally, move through all the regions of the face and head. Linger in the areas you know are usually tension spots for you.

- End, if you wish, by breathing through an imaginary "hole" in the top of your head, as if you were a whale. Let your breathing go through your entire body from one end to the other, as if it were flowing in through the top of the head and out through the toes, and back again. Finally, allow a moment of silence and stillness before getting up. Slowly move your hands and feet; feel the wholeness of your body again before returning to your day's routine.

- After completing the body tension scan, take two or three minutes to reflect. Enter the date in your Personal Log and record where you experienced tension or knotted muscles by answering these questions:

Where are the "hot spots," aches, or knots that are holding tension in my body?

_____

_____

_____

What events of the day or past weeks have brought on these aches or knots?

_____

_____

_____

What feelings do I associate with these events?

_____

_____

_____

What areas of my body are holding these emotions?

_____

_____

_____

Don't be concerned if you don't get a clear answer right away. Simply posing the questions raises awareness. To identify where and how your body holds emotions, keep a Personal Log for several weeks or months to see what patterns emerge.

THINGS TO WATCH FOR

- *Being "blocked" in a particular region of your body.*
  Let's say that each time you come to a certain area of the body—the knees, stomach, or shoulders, perhaps—you go numb, don't feel anything, or find you regularly skip that area and move on. This can be a common experience for someone who has experienced trauma, a serious injury, or physical or sexual abuse. It could be a signal that you have unresolved feelings or repressed memories that may need to be worked with and released.

- *Having difficulty because you are working with physical pain.*
  Serious pain in any part of your body may prevent you from concentrating. If this happens, continue to

move through the body, noting the sensations and thoughts that arise. As you reach the painful area, practice *moving through* the pain, experiencing it fully *in its turn* when you come to it.

If this is too difficult, stop scanning and just breathe in and out. Kabat-Zinn recommends imagining the in-breath penetrating into the tissue until it is completely absorbed, and the out-breath discharging or carrying away the pain. As you do this, try to notice how the sensations in the painful area change with each breath.

- *Finding it hard to maintain awareness because you fall asleep.*
  Falling asleep can provide important information about your body. Perhaps you are sleep-deprived, or maybe you are experiencing resistance to and discomfort about being in a state of awareness. It may mean you will have to give up some old emotional habits, like indulging in anger or blaming others for the unhappiness in your life. Avoidance and resistance are natural reactions to change and, if you persevere, need not become serious obstacles. Make note of any fears or resistance. Use them as grist for the learning mill, stepping-stones to going farther into the practice.

VARIATION: A QUICK BODY SCAN

Once you've become familiar with body scanning, quick versions of the practice will work. After mastering the technique, you can scan while on hold, caught in traffic, waiting for a light, riding the subway, or before going to sleep.

TRAIL MARKER

Pausing here, you can see that cultivating awareness is an unhurried, natural process that begins, like life itself, with the simple act of breathing. As you have been paying closer attention to the rhythm of your breath, you have developed greater sensitivity to the messages your body sends—clues to the patterns and habits of your emotional life. New insights about the connection between your mind and body emerge and reveal hidden truths about what you feel.

At this point, you may be experiencing the challenge of connecting deeply with yourself, especially if you are out of practice. Although you may be tempted to quickly move ahead, stay patient. Awareness will freely offer itself. In Kafka's words, "You don't need to leave your room. Remain sitting . . . and listen." Breathe. In moments of quietness and solitude, however brief, tune in. Your ability to do this well will assist you every step on this path toward personal change.

Now that the foundation of breathing is in place, you can move to the next step in the Establishments of Mindfulness: noticing and naming the wide range of feelings that are carried in your body, and recognizing your emotional habit-patterns.

CHAPTER 4

NAMING YOUR EXPERIENCE

Our minds go racing about like horses running wild in the fields, while our emotions remain unmanageable, like monkeys swinging in the trees.

DŌGEN ZENJI, 1237 C.E.[1]

When we pause and tune in to the body, we may experience the noise of a chattering mind, unsettled feelings, festering resentments, spinning "to do" lists, or scattered thoughts. The natural response of the human mind echoes the chaotic busyness of our world. To calm this inner cacophony, we need what psychologists call an "observing ego" or "second self."

I have an image of this second self as a kind of Jiminy Cricket from *Pinocchio*. He sits on your shoulder, whispers in your ear, and brings your attention to the swirl of feelings and thoughts that precede your actions and reactions. Naming our experience—listening to Jiminy's wise advice—gives us knowledge of and power over the emotions that hijack our thinking brain.

Physiologically, just naming our feelings activates the thinking brain's circuits, specifically the prefrontal lobes, allowing us to respond more effectively to stress. These prefrontal lobes act as a damper switch and release inhibitory neurons that stop the panic signals from the amygdala—like punching in a code that shuts down a security system's alarm.[2] In short, we *want* this part of our brain aware and activated so it can rein in our reactions.

The act of pausing to name our experience affects the situation immediately, providing several benefits:

- Negative feelings (built-up frustration, shame, regret, sadness, or fear) lose momentum, lessening their destructive power.

- Feelings no longer monopolize our consciousness.

- We are less likely to be swept into an amygdala hijack.

- We focus and calm down.

- We become less afraid of strong emotions.

- We recover more quickly from upset.

Once we know the *exact nature* of our feelings, we can handle them more effectively. In a study by University of Washington psychologist John Gottman, even the *act* of labeling emotions had a soothing effect on the nervous systems in children. Gottman's theory is ". . . that talking about an emotion as you are experiencing it engages the left lobe of the brain, which is the center of language and logic."[3]

The simple act of naming our emotions, and so re-engaging our thinking brain in the process, gives us some degree of control. We may still be traveling at high speed—feeling intense emotion—but we have, by naming, applied the brakes, slowed ourselves down. It isn't possible to stop our reaction entirely, but we have, perhaps, prevented a serious collision.

WHAT ARE WE NAMING?

There are three distinct kinds of emotional response:

- *Hot flashes or cold chills* are brief, strong experiences of emotion that flare for just seconds. Feeling precedes thought: Our face suddenly flushes with anger, our knees tremble, or our belly turns to mush.

- *Stewing and brewing* is the slower response that simmers in our thoughts before it leads to feeling. Here we replay the insult, nurse the injury, or recall the annoyance in our mind, spinning our mental wheels seeking a solution, frustrated anew, chastising ourselves for what we could have done. In this kind of emotional reaction, our thoughts themselves can trigger an amygdala hijack.

- *The past into the present.* There are times when our reaction in the present is blurred, when some triggering event—a scowl, condescending tone, or public affront—touches painful memories. The emotional mind reacts to the present *as though it were the past.*

  Early life experience such as prejudice, abuse, or betrayal can intensify this response. The amygdala has become hypervigilant, a hair trigger, ready to alert our survival responses at the slightest hint of harm. People left by a parent early in life through neglect, divorce, illness, or death, for instance, may be wary of abandonment in their adult relationships. Ever watchful, they are likely to overreact to small acts of forgetfulness as if they were intentional insults. Confirming their fears, they relive their past in the anticipation of abandonment in the present.

WHY DON'T WE NOTICE
OUR EMOTIONS?

Taking time to pause and note our feelings is no small task. Our days consist of ceaseless activity. Just trying to connect with our loved ones and maintain a measure of personal sanity is challenging enough.

We often get caught up in what others are doing *to us*—thinking about how to control *them*. Or it is easy to get tricked into thinking something "out there" will give us happiness. *If* only . . . *I had that new car, new house, new leather jacket, extended vacation, pay increase . . .* then *I would be content!*

In the midst of all this, how we are really feeling is akin to background music in a crowded elevator or the broadcast of a baseball game while we are washing the car. We only pay attention when a favorite oldie comes on, triggering some nostalgic thought; or maybe when the play-by-play announcer shouts, "Going . . . going . . . gone!"

Our emotions and the thoughts that provoke them murmur and sputter in the background of our awareness until they bubble up and burst out in an angry comment or leave us with an aching stomach. They live below the surface of our attention—complex, hidden, unconscious habits residing in the shadows of our mind until we glimpse within.

Bringing them to your awareness requires a gentle hand. Georgei Gurdjieff,[4] a teacher of mysticism in the early part of the twentieth century, gives us the following counsel:

Wild horses are neither trained by being left completely alone, nor by continual beating. Such measures will inevitably fail. We have to find a middle way. On one hand, no benefit comes from the negative attitude that it isn't worthwhile to try and train the wild horse at all. On the other hand, we have to accept that the horse is wild and have a compassionate approach towards training it. . . .

. . . Reins enable a rider to be aware of and influence a horse's movements, and to apply a little guidance where necessary. But if the rider pulls too hard, the horse may fight back. So at all times we aim for a balance between repressing the mind and giving it too much freedom. We learn to experience our thoughts in an accepting, uncontrived way; neither being too tense nor too loose. Thus our practice of mindfulness follows the wide and safe path—the middle way.

The practices that follow will help you find that way.

PRACTICING A DAILY EXAMEN

It might seem at first glance that our feelings are obvious; more thoughtful reflection reminds us of times we have been all too oblivious to what we really felt about something, or awoke to these feelings late in the game.

DANIEL GOLEMAN[5]

Doing a daily examen is a core practice in the Ignatian Spiritual Exercises, a sixteenth-century tradition of Christian contemplative prayer. I was drawn to the exercises after hearing of the parallels between modern twelve-step programs and this process for spiritual development written more than 450 years ago. For the next ten years I studied the exercises with Sister Mary Sharon Riley and the Sisters of the Cenacle in Chicago.

Iñigo de Oñaz y Loyola (1491–1556) developed these exercises during his transformation from a wealthy, arrogant soldier in the Spanish army to a revered spiritual leader. He was injured in the battle of Pamplona and spent months alone in a cave recovering before he could return home. During these months, he reflected on the "diverse 'voices' inside of him—to the movements of consolation and desolation in his heart and spirit."[6] He came out of the cave a changed man, and people wanted to know what had happened, what he had done, and how his insight could help them. As a relatively uneducated layman, he wrote down his methods, and they have endured for centuries. Iñigo went on to found the Jesuit Order and is now known as Saint Ignatius of Loyola.

The "daily examen of consciousness" is the rich and deep practice of pausing to take note of the movements of our heart—our emotions—and, most importantly, which of these we should act on. It is a practice that cultivates awareness, where "you can grow more sensitive to your own spirit—its longings, its powers, its Source."[7]

What follows is an adaptation of this practice—taking a regular inventory of our feeling life and naming our inner experience *accurately*.

The range of human emotion is vast and subtle, a rich palette portraying our life experience. There are more nuances than words to capture this range: fiery hues of anger or rage; the blue mood of sorrow or loss; the dull gray of indifference; vibrancy in exuberance and joy; softer shades of contentment or gratitude.

Naming our experience, with its many emotional

intricacies, helps us calm ourselves in the midst of an intense reaction.

PRACTICE

DOING A DAILY EXAMEN

This practice asks you to spend ten minutes at the end of each day reflecting on the emotions you experienced that day.

WHAT YOU'LL NEED

- About ten minutes at the end of your day for about two weeks.

- A quiet, private place to reflect.

- Your Personal Log.

TRY THIS

- Review the Daily Examen Checklist that follows. The checklist groups feelings by color to reflect the palette of emotions we experience in life.

- At the end of each day, look through the list and put a checkmark next to the three to five feelings that were the most memorable to you that day. (If you experience others not on the list, write them at the bottom of the chart.)

- To become well versed in naming your emotions, continue noting your feelings each day for at least two weeks. Take a break for a few days and then resume the practice for another two weeks. (When you use the checklist provided, you may want to make a copy of the checklist or use a different-colored pen for each week.)

- When you've practiced for about four weeks in a two-month period, review your checklist. What patterns emerge? Take some quiet time to reflect and write down answers to these questions in your Personal Log:

What emotions do I experience regularly?

_____

_____

_____

Are there particular emotions that I rarely or almost never feel?

_____

_____

_____

How do I act or react when I experience these feelings?

_____

_____

_____

How does this reaction affect my important relationships?

_____

_____

_____

What does this suggest about my emotional habits?

_____

_____

_____

DAILY EXAMEN CHECKLIST						
	Monday	Tuesday	Wednesday	Thursday	Friday	Sat./Sun.
RED PALETTE						
Anger						
Irritation						
Resentment						
Hatred						
YELLOW PALETTE						
Happiness						
Pride						
Satisfaction						
Desire						
Love						
Loved						
Gratitude						
BLUE PALETTE						
Hurt						
Sadness						
Grief						
Regret						

DAILY EXAMEN CHECKLIST						
	Monday	Tuesday	Wednesday	Thursday	Friday	Sat./Sun.
GREEN PALETTE						
Anxiety						
Apprehension						
Edginess						
Concern						
Envy						
GRAY PALETTE						
Disgust						
Shame						
Guilt						
Depression						
Self-pity						
OTHER FEELINGS						
Other . . .						
Other . . .						

THINGS TO WATCH FOR

- *You can't identify a particular feeling.*
  Developing an emotional vocabulary will take a while—particularly if you are not accustomed to tuning in to your feelings or specifying more subtle emotions. Struggling to pinpoint your feelings can also be a signal that certain emotions are "not acceptable" because of your culture or upbringing. While working with a group of clients in the Pacific Rim, I noticed that every "negative" emotion was described with the same expression. Anger, sadness, anxiety, and shame were all "upset"—the result of strong cultural norms that prohibited such expression.

  If this is true for you, stay with the practice of a daily examen for a longer time. Simply asking yourself the question *What am I feeling today?* gives permission for furthering emotional self-knowledge, even if you don't have the answer right away. Also, the next practice, Sitting in Meditation, may help to deepen your awareness.

- *You have the same feeling come up time and time again.*
  Maybe your checklist has sadness or envy checked day after day. It may indicate that you are going through a troubling time—a lover is absent in body or spirit, a child goes to college leaving an empty nest, a parent is aging or ill. In some cases, it may be entirely fitting to have these feelings. On the other hand, it may be a clear sign that you are caught in an emotional habit that needs to change.

Beginning in childhood and throughout life, we acquire our emotional habits and the thoughts and actions that go with them. As we use those neural path-

ways over and over, they eventually turn into the equivalent of neural highways in the brain. The underlying
circuitry makes habitual emotional response easier, particularly when we are tired, under pressure, or in the
throes of an amygdala hijack.

It takes compassion, time, and commitment to
change our habits and form new, more emotionally
intelligent neural pathways. And it *can* be done, with
the right practice.

NOTICING YOUR FEELINGS IN THE MOMENT

In us, there is a river of feelings, in which every drop of
water is a different feeling, and each feeling relies on all
the others for its existence. To observe it, we just sit on
the bank of the river and identify each feeling as it sur-
faces, flows by, and disappears.

THICH NHAT HANH[8]

This simple, powerful practice uses mindful breathing
to explore feelings that arise as we sit quietly. Alone or
combined with the upcoming practices in chapter 5,
Accepting What You Feel, it has helped me transcend
the turbulent and upsetting emotions I find most debilitating: fear, hatred, and shame.

Drawing on the guidance from ancient texts in
Mahayana Buddhism, this practice tells us to sit,
breathe, and "feel the feelings *in* the feelings" as a

method for deepening our awareness and freeing us from distress.

The following passage, revered as pure teaching from the ancestors, was first taught by Gautama Buddha in his mother tongue—Ardhamagadhi—then passed from generation to generation through oral tradition, and finally recorded in Pali script, a dialect used in western India. It has been translated to English and given to us by the modern teacher and scholar Thich Nhat Hanh.

> Whenever the practitioner has a pleasant feeling, he is aware, "I am experiencing a pleasant feeling." Whenever he has a painful feeling, he is aware, "I am experiencing a painful feeling." Whenever he experiences a feeling that is neither pleasant nor painful, he is aware, "I am experiencing a neutral feeling." Trying to get rid of our feelings is just another form of fantasy.[9]

And so we learn to sit. Breathing. Listening to the wind and the rustle of our thoughts. Letting them go. Listening to the wind and the gurgling of emotions. Doing nothing, for now, nothing to resist.

PRACTICE

SITTING IN MEDITATION

This practice asks you to complete a ten- to fifteen-minute meditation that can be done walking, sitting, or lying down. Sitting usually provides maximum concentration unless a physical difficulty prevents or counterindicates this posture.

The exploratory questions in this practice were given to me by Dosho Port-sensei, guiding teacher at Clouds in Water Zen Center in St. Paul, Minnesota. He is a dharma heir[8] of Dainin Katagiri-roshi,[9] a central figure in bringing Zen Buddhism to the West.

WHAT YOU'LL NEED

- Fifteen to twenty minutes to complete this practice.

- A quiet place to walk, sit, or lie down. For sitting meditation, use a chair or sit on the floor so that your body is relaxed and your spine is straight. Or, if you're lying down, make sure you're in a comfortable position where you can breathe easily and keep an alert mind.

- Your Personal Log.

TRY THIS

(For the purpose of providing clear instructions, this practice focuses on working with fear. If you are working with another negative or afflictive emotion, substitute that emotion for "fear" in this activity.)

- For the first two or three minutes, practice mindful breathing. As you breathe, bring your body into harmony with the breath by saying to yourself, *Breathing in, I know that I feel fear. Breathing out, I know that I feel fear.* Then, only *In, fear* with your in-breath and *Out, fear* with your out-breath.

- Next, allow yourself to experience the sensations of fear in your body. Gently visit the physical sensations of fear by thinking about the following questions, lingering a minute or two to let your intuition or imagination give you the answer.

~ *Where in my body do I feel fear?*

~ *What is its shape?*

~ *How big is it?*

~ *Does it have a color?*

~ *What is its temperature?*

~ *Is it solid or hollow?*

~ *Does it travel to other areas of my body?*

Try to stay with this exploration of "feelings in the feelings" for at least ten minutes.

- Then, having thoroughly "felt your fear with bare attention," complete the meditation with several minutes of breathing, calming the fear and letting it go by saying, *Breathing in, calming fear. Breathing out, calming fear.* Then: *In, calming fear* with the in-breath and *Out, calming fear* with the out-breath. Here, you stay with your emotion and become calm *at the same time*—without disregarding or repressing the emotion. Allow yourself to feel fear *and* be calm, side by side, in the same moment.

- When you have completed your period of sitting meditation, you may want to take one or two final minutes to record your reflections and insights in your Personal Log.

THINGS TO WATCH FOR

- *Various thoughts and worries interfere with the meditation.* Meditation does not involve forcing anything, such as pushing thoughts away to quiet the mind. We seek

and walk the "middle way" with these practices.
Gently and firmly bring your attention back to the
breath whenever you find yourself wandering. Then
return to the question that you were answering when
you drifted away and pick up the meditation from
that point.

- *Some of your emotions have been "packed away" for some time.*

  Although calling our emotions by name and experiencing them fully can have a calming effect, some of
  our emotions may have been "in storage" for a long
  time. If you are working with old, repressed feelings,
  you may want to seek out a professional psychologist,
  a counselor, guiding teacher, or spiritual director to
  support you. When you are opening up old emotional wounds, it is important to go slowly and cultivate awareness over time.

T R A I L   M A R K E R

At this rest stop, you are midway in the exploration of
the Self. From this vantage point, you can see the depth
and richness and activity of your emotional life. You
have examined the range and palette of your many feelings—from the brightness of joy to the blue sorrow of
grief to the ashy smolder of resentment. This process of
self-discovery could be compared to putting a drop of
ocean water under a microscope. Where before there

was only water, now you see an elaborate world teeming with life.

Naming your experience has awakened your thinking brain to its partner the emotional brain, and strengthened your capacity to develop an observing self. With each footstep, you are uncovering more of who you are and what governs your reactions in the world—crucial knowledge for determining your future course.

Take this moment to survey your emotional landscape—what you have learned on the journey thus far. Note the highlights in your Personal Log:

What key tension spots in my body alert me that I am "heating up," warning me of an impending amygdala hijack?

_____

_____

_____

_____

_____

_____

What themes have come to light while practicing the Daily Examen and Sitting Meditation?

_____

_____

_____

_____

_____

_____

*What have I learned about my emotional habits—those
"same old paths" I go down when I am triggered?*

_____

_____

_____

_____

_____

_____

Hold these insights in your mind as you take the next
step in your journey of awareness: *accepting* what you
feel, what you have named, what *is*. Succeeding in
changing your emotional habits depends on—first—
accepting who you are in this moment, right here, right
now. This alone may be a profound shift, opening pathways of greater compassion for yourself and, ultimately,
others.

And so, after this brief rest, let us move on to deeper
realms of the Self.

CHAPTER 5

ACCEPTING WHAT YOU FEEL

Let nothing disturb you, nothing cause you fear; all things pass.

TERESA OF AVILA[1]

Even when we *tune in* and accurately *name* our emotions, we may still find ways to quash or ignore what arises unless we learn to *accept:* feel without denying, judging, or being swept away by our emotions.

Too often, we needle ourselves about our feelings: *I shouldn't be angry; Only sissies get scared; Get over it; Maybe if I get busy, it will go away; Be happy.* Censoring our reactions or masking our true feelings traps our emotions. They simmer under the surface and bubble over in head throbs of resentment or sleepless nights of self-criticism. We don't want to admit that we feel hatred, or are capable of being vicious, so we banish those feelings to the dark corners of the mind, never to be examined in the light of our awareness.

The difficulties we have accepting disruptive emotions can often be traced to our personal and cultural history. Our early experiences form an emotional legacy, etching the neural pathways that determine our moods and shape our feelings. As children, we absorb what is modeled at home and incorporate those examples into our emotional repertoire. We learn *This is anger,* and whether it is "bad" or "good." We learn *This is loneliness,* and wonder if we can be cherished. We see how to act under duress or when enjoying prosperity. We learn to take or give in relationships—which emotions to heed, which to disregard.

With time and effort we can alter the effects of our emotional past by reshaping the emotional habits that no longer serve us, while keeping those we value. Tolerating painful feelings, *accepting* them rather than judging them as "good" or "bad," loosens their hold on us. We can learn to weather blustering emotions without acting on them. Determining an appropriate action comes later.

For now, we have the critical work of appreciating our emotions and ourselves—not always an easy thing to do. We may uncover some things that at first are "ugly" or troubling. An upsurge of afflictive feelings—if we have the comfort and protection of support—will pass. If we accept our "negative" feelings, they actually lighten in time. In fact, we aren't really free to experience happiness or joy if we are storing old, destructive emotions.

I remember vividly my own struggles in learning not to judge myself, deny my feelings, or let them carry me away. In my twenties, seeking solace, I decided to spend a year living in a monastery called Nada in northern Arizona.

The monastery, founded by a Carmelite monk as an experiment in returning to the simplicity and solitude of ascetic life, provided a "Christian Zen" approach to spiritual development. We lived in hermitages, kept silence, and spent days studying, walking, working, and meditating. I lived with a bed, sink, chair, desk, lamp, and hot plate for cooking. Meals were simple and bland.

Though looking for inner calm, I was not peaceful there. Hours, days, and weeks passed with only the noise of my own mind. Anger and jealousy arose. Old memories would stir—slights and resentments, losses and loneliness, sorrow and grief, and pangs of a wounded heart. My inner voice had a sharp, nasty edge: *Whatever made you think you could meditate away your troubles? You are so stupid! Lazy, too—all you do is fall asleep and stumble around . . . pretending to be holy.*

This was not what I'd come for. I wanted serenity. I wanted to rise above my shortcomings and float on the clouds in a feathery peace. I was discouraged and felt like a failure.

Father Michael—the scruffy-bearded spiritual director with thick glasses and a plaid shirt over his robe—responded to my troubles with a kind, humble voice, twinkling with humor as he told me the story of Jesus rubbing mud on the eyelids of a blind man. "You have a distorted way of seeing, Thérèse," he said. "You are harsh, unrealistic in your expectations. Don't avoid what burdens you. Grieve deeply and it will pass. Live in the present moment and you will find joy and sorrow rising together. You can be alive in your sadness; let the mud fall from your eyes."

He suggested that I walk. And so I began to wander and sing in the quiet acceptance of the desert. After many weeks surrounded by its twisted, scarred, and prickly beauty, I found my own voice. If sadness arose, I invented a sad song. Free to acknowledge what I had previously subdued, I felt moments of sweetness break through. Alone in the desert, my own voice sounded angry notes, tearful hums, or merry tunes. Just me.

By simply letting these feelings roll out—without doing harm to anyone—I loosened up. I was amazed to discover that anger *and* happiness *and* sorrow could exist all in one breath, in the same moment. My experience with accepting my emotions was kind of like frostbite, though—it stings as you thaw. Judging, suppressing, or hiding "negative" emotions lends only temporary relief. Our feelings are likely to leak out in physical symptoms or intolerance of others.

Accepting the uncensored me, I discovered that the grief from early experiences lessened. Prior to my time at Nada, much of my childhood pain was packed away— blank spots in my memory. I didn't *want* to remember. Heartbreaks from broken relationships subsided. I realized I was more than my feelings and that accepting them didn't shatter me. It's a strange comfort to realize that emotions just *are.* If you trust them, they wash through, leaving you stronger, allowing joy to return.

We can't move forward or change for the better until we accept who we are in this moment. The following practices are designed to bring about this change.

EXPLORING YOUR EMOTIONAL LEGACY

A man wearing a T-shirt and jeans followed his wife out into the driveway, screaming at her in front of the reticent but curious neighbors about how she was handling their teenaged son. After she drove off, he raged at the walls and into the empty rooms of the house.

Later that day, his embarrassed son confronted him about his behavior. They yelled at each other until his son shoved him in frustration. The father called the police and had him taken to juvenile detention. At the hearing, the court referee ordered the son to take a class in anger management.

The father thought involving the police would stop the cycle of anger and abuse that had gone on with his own father, but he refused to go to the class with his son, saying, "I don't need a class and I don't *have a problem with anger."*

Our families—for better or worse—shape our emotional lives. What we see, hear, and feel in our formative years stays with us, whether our lives were turbulent or relatively smooth. However we grew up, vestiges of the past remain.

This practice invites you to reflect on what you learned about emotions while growing up. It will ask you how your parents or key caregivers expressed their feelings, what their actions taught you, and the resulting effects on your own emotional life. We can't change the past, but we *can* see its imprint and accept it. As we gain greater compassion for ourselves, we begin to turn around debilitating emotional habits, retreading our old neural pathways.

PRACTICE

REFLECTING ON YOUR EMOTIONAL HABITS

In this practice, you'll first identify how your parents or other key caregivers expressed their feelings, and then heighten your awareness of how their emotional habits have influenced your own.

WHAT YOU'LL NEED

- Twenty to thirty minutes to complete the practice.

- A quiet place to reflect and write.
- Your Personal Log.

TRY THIS

- After reflecting on each question below, write your response in your Personal Log. If nothing comes to mind for one of the questions, let it go and return to it at another time. Also, asking siblings or relatives to help you recall your family's emotional life can give you further insight.

How did my mother [or father, or caregiver] *show anger, sadness, grief, pleasure, happiness, and dissatisfaction?*

_____

_____

_____

_____

How did my mother [or father, or caregiver] *respond when I was angry, sad, afraid, disappointed, or elated?*

_____

_____

_____

_____

Who was there when I came home from school? What kinds of questions did they ask about my day?

_____

_____

_____

_____

Whom did I turn to when I was disappointed, had unpleasant surprises, great news, or happy events?

_____

_____

_____

How did my mother and father [or caregivers] *handle conflict between themselves?*

_____

_____

_____

[If you had siblings] *How did our parents handle conflict between us?*

_____

_____

_____

• Next, reflect on what your caregivers' actions taught you and how that has affected your own emotional habits. Record the answers to the following questions in your Personal Log.

How has my mother's [or other important caregiver's] *style of expressing or not expressing anger, fear, sadness, or joy affected the way I express my own feelings?*

_____

_____

~ I reflect my mother's style of expressing [name a feeling] *by . . .*

_____

_____

_____

How has my father's [or other important caregiver's]
*style of expressing or not expressing anger, fear, sadness, or
joy affected the way I express myself today?*

_____

_____

_____

~ I reflect my father's style of expressing [name a feeling]
by . . .

_____

_____

_____

*What particular emotions were absent or hidden in my
family?*

_____

_____

_____

*~ I would like to change this pattern of expressing or not
expressing* [name emotion] *by . . .*

_____

_____

_____

- In the next few days and weeks, notice how your
  emotional habits affect your actions and reactions.
  You may want to note the date and time, and give a
  brief description of one or two revealing incidents in
  your Personal Log.

OBSERVING, IDENTIFYING, AND ACCEPTING YOUR FEELINGS

In this practice, we work to accept our feelings as they *are*. All of them—"the good, the bad, and the ugly." Without judgment, blame, or criticism. We welcome them like an old friend. They are part of us, an emotional family member.

The problem is that many of us don't like certain feelings. We may think, *But I don't want anger to be an old friend! I want it to be a stranger.* And this is just the point; we cannot banish our negative feelings. Repressing them ensures that they will come back to haunt us: bubble up, boil over, or surface in a physical symptom.

Instead, we invite them into our awareness. And then we gently observe, identify, and accept them. Nothing more. For now, that is enough.

A client told me how she worked with this practice:

One rainy autumn day, I got caught up in a blizzard of falling leaves until the breeze quieted and they fluttered down in a chaotic dance of color—golden aspen, red maple, amber elm—to the cold gray sidewalk.

Later I thought that accepting what we feel is like standing still with our emotions swirling like the leaves, just noticing the spectrum of colors and contrasts—bright yellows and reds, drab browns. Some stunning and some dull, the brilliant blend of nature. We pause in their midst and say, Hello crimson anger, hello brilliant yellow joy, copper fear, orange irritation, drab brown disgust, violet grief.

Standing still, seeing all the color, leaves settling over the path, I took a step forward and moved on.

Seeing the full range of our emotions as natural helps us accept them without being swept up in their drama.

PRACTICE

WELCOMING YOUR FEELINGS LIKE AN OLD FRIEND

I learned this meditation from the venerable Thich Nhat Hanh, while on retreat with him in upstate New York. It instructs us to welcome our feelings—invite them in, ask them to pull up a chair and visit for a while, have some tea—as we would an old friend. We get to know them and accept them as part of us. We can allow them in, touch them, let them go. We don't have to act on them. This is the wisdom of the practice.

WHAT YOU'LL NEED

- Ten to twenty minutes to complete the practice.

- A quiet place to sit or lie down. For sitting meditation, sit in a chair or on the floor so that your body is relaxed and your spine is straight. If you lie down, make sure you're in a comfortable position where you can breathe easily and keep an alert mind.

- Your Personal Log.

TRY THIS

- Begin this meditation with five minutes of mindful breathing.

- Take the next few moments to recognize each feeling as it arises (for example, look at your guilt and recognize it as guilt). This is the practice of "feeling the feelings in the feelings."

- Let the feeling be. In the words of Thich Nhat Hanh, "It is best not to say, 'Go away, Fear. I don't like you. You are not me.' It is much more effective to say, 'Hello, Fear. How are you today?' Doing this may not be easy at first, but remember that you are more than just your feelings. As long as mindfulness is present, you will not drown in your feeling. In fact, you begin transforming it in the very moment you give birth to awareness in yourself."[2]

- Take the next five to ten minutes to visit with your emotions: anxiety, anger, self-pity, fear, worry, boredom, shame, or whatever feeling arises. Ask them to pull up a chair and stay awhile.

- Linger here with your imagination for a few moments. Picture the emotion in your mind's eye.

  ~ *What is its face?*

  ~ *How is it dressed?*

  ~ *Where in my house does it come to sit?*

  ~ *What does it have to say?*

  ~ *What would I like to ask it?*

  ~ *How do I feel about having it as my guest?*

Notice what you learn about this emotion and turn your concentration to accepting it, warmly and graciously, despite its muddy feet, rude manners, or threatening face. *Oh, I know you. You are familiar, an old friend. How are you today?*

- Now, complete the meditation with five minutes of breathing, calming, and letting go. You can do this by saying to yourself, *Breathing in, I calm myself. Breathing out, I smile.* Then: *In, calm* with the in-breath and *Out, smile* with the out-breath.

Take a few moments to jot down your emerging thoughts and images in your Personal Log. Repeating this practice over time reduces the size and "ugliness" of the emotions we find most distressing.

TRAIL MARKER

This past leg of the trail has taken you through the melting snow of self-acceptance. You have seen the footprints of your early family life in the muddy path, noticing their imprint on your emotional legacy and the ways it affects your reactions day to day. This heritage is ingrained in your neural pathways, likely to emerge when you are tired or stressed or in the throes of an amygdala hijack.

Rather than close your eyes to what has shaped you, and so become its victim, you have embraced it in the sweetness of compassion for yourself. Honoring your history by allowing it to be a source of understanding yourself frees you from its hold. Now you can keep the best of your past and still change the things that interfere with what you want in life.

Rather than deny your emotions, diminish their importance, or admonish their source, you can now welcome them as old friends—without fear or shame. Accepting painful or negative feelings lightens them, making us less likely to be swept away in their drama. We are more free to choose how to act in spite of their wind and roar, able to better harness their energy for courage or joy.

You turn now toward the final and most fertile step in investigating the Self—looking at the root causes of your emotional reactions, observing the thought patterns that poison your happiness. As you travel, stay wrapped in the warmth of self-acceptance, and as you look deeply, "Let nothing disturb you, nothing cause you fear."

CHAPTER 6

LOOKING DEEPLY

> Until we can cleanse ourselves of inner confusion and
> penetrate the various layers of the mind, our judgment
> and actions will only reflect our inherent restlessness,
> like bees trapped in a jar.
>
> TARTHANG TULKU RINPOCHE[1]

This final step in cultivating mindfulness requires us to
investigate our thoughts. Although sometimes a difficult process, it can light the way through the dark val-
leys, the recesses of our innermost self. Here, we dig
down and discover what lies beneath, understanding
that "our own psychology and physiology are present in
the roots of any feeling."[2]

Our past experiences, present circumstances, and
future desires alter our perspective of the world and
ourselves. When discovering root causes, we find our
reactions are more about *us* than another person. Like
wearing blue-, yellow-, gray-, or rose-tinted sunglasses,
our ideas and expectations filter and color our view. We
see the world and other people through our mental
models—our lenses. Some perspectives enhance our
vision; others cloud it with anger, restlessness, or fear.

Say your life has been marked by the false promises
of loved ones. You might react with anger to a colleague
who fails to finish an important report on time, calling

her "unprofessional and incompetent" in a blistering e-mail. You later recoil in horror as you read what you wrote: ". . . your busiest day is a stroll in the park compared to the amount of work I do before nine. And still, you cannot meet a simple deadline." When you find out that she missed that deadline because of a last-minute request from the vice president, you cringe. You jumped to a conclusion because the present situation sparked the memory of past slights.

Our thought habits, too, result from deeply ingrained neuropathways. They determine what we pay attention to, how we interpret and explain what happens to us. The same external event can look different depending on our lenses, our view.

Consider this ancient Chinese folktale:

A country man lost his axe. Suspecting that his neighbor's son had stolen it, he started observing the young man closely. It seemed that both his manner of walking and his tone of voice were different from the ordinary person. All in all, his every act and movement resembled those of a thief.

Later, he found the lost axe himself. As it turned out, he had dropped it in the valley where he went to chop wood. The next day, he came across his neighbor's son again. Only this time when he carefully observed his manner of walking and listened to his tone of voice, he found that neither resembled that of a thief.[3]

In addition to external triggers, negative images *inside* us can escalate an amygdala hijack. Our own thoughts become mini triggers for the amygdala, building on each other, setting off surge after surge of stress hormones to the body. Worried thoughts can

become an endless loop, spiraling us farther and farther downward into negativity—how tired we feel, how
little energy we have, how little work we're getting
done, who hasn't returned our phone calls. Brooding
begets brooding. The more we think about what angers
us, the angrier we become.

I remember a sleepless night drinking tea on the
back porch, rehashing a project gone awry with a major
corporate client and flashing back on a colleague's false
smile, her mocking voice informing me that I was "no
longer needed." I sat, replaying the rumors and attacks
on my credibility, the deliberate deceptions about
meeting times and deadlines. Betrayed, ashamed, and
searching for what I had done wrong, I felt threatened
by this baptism by fire in the hardball world of corporate politics. I couldn't let it go, and this was three
months later. Alone with the moon and crickets, I
reacted to the incident as if it had just happened yes-
terday.

In fact, how we think about and explain our experiences to ourselves is so crucial that it can make a difference between health and illness. In a study by Martin
Seligman, a psychologist at the University of Pennsyl-
vania,[4] pessimistic thinking was shown to increase risk
of physical illness and depression. More recent discoveries support the powerful connection between mind
and body, establishing how "states of mind can affect
the strength of the immune system and the robustness
of the cardiovascular system."[5]

In an analysis of more than one hundred studies,
Howard Friedman at the University of California—
Irvine found that "those who tended to be unusually
hostile and angry, very anxious, sad, pessimistic, or
tense, had double the risk of getting a serious illness,

including asthma, chronic headaches, stomach ulcers, heart disease, and arthritis."[6] In another study, people who are "repressors"—those who deny their feelings— were shown to be more susceptible to diseases like asthma, high blood pressure, and colds.[7] A multitude of research provides evidence that our thoughts have an undeniable effect on our health.

In fact, our thought habits form a kind of "portable stage set"[8] that we carry with us. Whatever the situation, we re-create the drama of past experience and read the scene in a way that affirms our existing worldview. If we hold the mental script of an innocent victim, we may constantly feel "done to" and blame others for our troubles. Or, if our trust has been broken time and again, we may approach the world with suspicion and fear, expecting betrayal. Then again, we may see opportunity in a setback and rise to the challenge, invigorated and open to new interpretations. Our own thought habits— our *internal* formations—cast the scene.

Our goal is to investigate our thoughts and recognize how they arrange our world. When we become aware of these "objects of the mind," patterns begin to emerge. We discover how our habits lean toward tragedy, comedy, or satire.

By again turning to the ancient Sutra on the Establishments of Mindfulness, we find the way to retread the pathways of destructive thoughts—honing new, more emotionally intelligent roads for the mind to follow. It instructs us to observe the "objects of our mind" with the same careful attention we gave to scanning the body for tension spots and noting our feelings in a daily examen. Here we follow our wandering minds, uncover our objects of desire, and discern our real cares and concerns.

Flashes of anger, dissatisfaction, and self-delusion are part of the human condition, but there is a difference between these normal human responses and the persistent moods or mind-sets that "tilt" the mind and regularly trigger the amygdala. Gautama Buddha said there are certain unhealthy "fetters" or "knots" in the mind, binding us, causing us to suffer, preventing freedom and peace of mind.

A knot is an ingrained thinking habit, a recurring theme in our perceptions, a tinted lens in our mind that colors and distorts our view. Buddha said the knots of strong anger, craving, and delusion are particularly troublesome. He called them "poisons of the mind." I think of them as bees trapped in a jar.

PRACTICES

 INVESTIGATING THE POISONS OF THE MIND

This practice is an exercise in peeling back our strong reactions to their root by discovering the primary feelings buried under the surface of our awareness. By looking at the ways these knots appear in your thoughts and actions, you can—with some effort—discover their origin.

STRONG ANGER: THE HORNETS OF THE MIND

Strong anger stems from perceptions that *exaggerate the negative* aspects of another person or situation. Instead of seeing others in a natural light, we take a dim view— disapproving, critical, intolerant. We tend to amplify minor mistakes or irritating mannerisms. This outlook shades and clouds the way we look at others and, in turn, the way they see us—a self-perpetuating, vicious cycle of distortion.

You may be caught in a knot of anger if, over a period of weeks or months, you *frequently:*[9]

- [ ] Think everyone but you is stupid.

- [ ] Blame others when you are unhappy.

- [ ] Envy others' good fortune.

- [ ] Feel intolerant and impatient with other people.

- [ ] Blame others when you don't get what you want.

- [ ] Have harsh, critical thoughts about yourself or others.

- [ ] Derive a secret pleasure about the misfortunes of those you don't like.

- [ ] Compose and refine a blistering speech to someone who has angered you.

- [ ] Rationalize mean actions, thinking, *They had it coming.*

- [ ] Plan to get even with someone you think has wronged you, and hope for opportunities to carry it out.

- [ ] Wish harm would come to someone you don't like.

- [ ] Hold on to past resentments or keep a running list of past slights, grievances, and hurts.

When under the influence of recurring thoughts of strong anger, we exaggerate and attach permanence to the displeasing characteristics of others. We want to strike back. "Anger is like a flame blazing up and consuming our self-control, making us think, say, and do things that we will probably regret later."[10]

Though persistent anger affects our happiness, suppressing it only delays an often inevitable reaction. Instead, we need to become aware of angry urges as they *first* enter the mind. With an early glimpse—in the gentle light of awareness—we can better see their root, observe with mindfulness, and refrain from judgment.

Only then can we come to accept our feelings without indulging in destructive behavior, stinging others, or turning on ourselves in bitter self-criticism. We can etch healthier, more effective neural pathways by channeling our angry urges into assertiveness, compassion, or forgiveness—antidotes for old, poisonous mental habits.

CRAVING: THE HONEYBEES OF THE MIND

Craving, the root of envy, *exaggerates the attractiveness* of another person or thing. We project an embellished image, cling to it, yearn for it, and want to possess the apparently beautiful object we have constructed in our imagination. We overestimate the amount of satisfaction or fulfillment we would have "if only" we could get what we want.

You may be caught in a knot of craving if, over a period of weeks or months you are *often:*[11]

☐ Getting lost, absorbed in fantasies of the "ideal relationship."

☐ Wanting to have more, more, more—possessions, friends, parties, food, status, and so forth.

☐ Reliving past pleasurable experiences.

☐ Longing for the object of your desire.

☐ Desperately wanting someone to fall in love with you.

☐ Believing you "can't be happy" or your "life can't move on" until you get what you want.

☐ Being selfish or stingy—thinking if you give warmth, comfort, or help, there will not be enough left for you.

☐ Wanting lots of options—the television on in one room, music in another, a sandwich in the kitchen, a friend on the telephone, all while doing housework.

☐ Thinking you *have* to have that new car, new outfit, new home, new furniture.

☐ Comparing yourself to others or feeling superior to those around you.

☐ Justifying your cravings.

☐ Looking for a way to lie, bend, or break the rules to get what you want.

Craving is about acquisition, accumulation, and holding on. The more we crave, the more we think about what we don't have. The more we focus on what we don't have, the more we want. In the words of the Tibetan master Gyalua Tsongkhapa (1357–1419), founder of the Gelugpa sect of Buddhism and first Dalai Lama,

> . . . Just as it is difficult to remove an oil stain from a cotton cloth, in the same way, this hankering after and getting more involved with the *thing* [one wants] makes it very difficult to get rid of.[12]

Cravings for more possessions, the affections of a certain person, more status, and more power often result in restlessness, discontent, and further stress. The amygdala is triggered into fears of "not having." The antidote to this mental knot—the new pathway—is to turn the yearning for temporary fulfillment into a desire for deeper, more lasting happiness.

DELUSION: THE DRUNKEN BEES OF THE MIND

Where strong anger undervalues and craving overvalues, delusion *simply ignores*. Based on the mistaken belief that ignorance is bliss, our delusional filters prevent us from seeing the obvious. We simply do not recognize the mental distortions inherent in our thinking habits.

You may be caught in a knot of delusion if, over a period of weeks or months, you *often*:[13]

☐ Insist you are right.

☐ Change the subject, watch television, or stay busy to avoid feeling.

☐ Affect a *Why bother* or *Don't know, don't care* attitude.

☐ Ignore opinions different from yours or think of people who are not like you as deficient or wrong.

☐ Believe problems or responsibilities will just go away if you don't think about them.

☐ Worry and fret instead of taking necessary action.

☐ Repeat poor choices over and over.

☐ Forget important commitments you have made to others or make excuses for not following through on promises.

☐ Feel drowsy and uneasy in the face of criticism.

☐ Think *You're wrong* or *You don't really understand me* when another person confronts you about something you've done.

☐ Are unaware of your conduct (body, speech, and mind) or remain oblivious to the consequences of your actions.

☐ Use alcohol, other mind-altering chemicals, sex, television, and the like to numb yourself and escape from painful emotions.

If you discover a knot while observing your mind, gently accept it. Rather than pulling and tightening, acceptance helps us work the knot free.

In "observing the objects of the mind," we look deeply to see how we are exaggerating—in fact, often *imagining*—the positive or negative in another person or situation. And after we investigate our delusions and notice their consequences, we can change how we act with those we love.

By looking deeply, we find that the source of our pain often lies *inside* us. Although another person's actions may have *triggered* our amygdala-driven response, the true source of our reaction is *our* strong anger, *our* craving, and *our* deluded thoughts.

SO HOW DO WE LOOK DEEPLY? WHAT DO WE NEED TO DO?

We look for the causes within ourselves so we can acknowledge them as our own, getting at the roots of our perceptions, questioning the thoughts that trigger our responses, feelings, and reactions. Further, we look at the influence of our emotional memory, asking, *What has been triggered in me? What "match" has the amygdala found? What part of my perception may be based on partial or limited information?* Though this inquiry may seem difficult (given our natural, human resistance), thousands of years of practice by generations of people before us have shown us it *can* learn to recognize our misconceptions and see how they filter our views from day to day.

Like tuning in to the body, or identifying our moods, here we observe our *thoughts* as they enter, fill, and leave our mind. This practice of "observing the objects of the mind" is the final discipline recommended in the ancient Sutra on the Establishments of Mindfulness— completing the cycle of deepening awareness in body, heart, and mind.

If we don't penetrate the layers of our mind, we will stay restless, agitated, trapped. By looking deeply, we release the antidotes to the poisons of the mind.

 ASKING FIVE WHYS

This practice asks you to reflect on your day or week, pinpoint a strong feeling or reaction, and ask a series of five *why* questions to discover the underlying cause or root distortion of the mental knot.

WHAT YOU'LL NEED

- About fifteen to twenty minutes of uninterrupted time.

- A quiet, private place to think and reflect.

- Your Personal Log.

TRY THIS

- At the end of your day, sit down in a quiet, private place and think about a troublesome feeling or reaction you've experienced that day. Pinpoint one feeling or reaction to investigate more deeply.

- Describe (two to three sentences here or in your Personal Log) the situation that triggered your strong feeling or reaction.

What triggered my reaction?

_____

_____

_____

What did I say or do?

_____

_____

_____

- Now compose, reflect, and respond to a series of at least five *why* questions. The goal is to "peel back" your reaction, layer by layer, until you expose its root cause—uncovering *why* you feel and respond the way you do.

  For example, you could start with a general *why* question, such as:

  ~ *Why did I react so strongly to that character in the film [the novel, the class, and so forth]?*

  ~ *Why do I feel uncomfortable or angry when I hear someone say that?*

  ~ *Why did I respond as I did?*

- Then continue asking *why* several more times, probing deeper with each question. Begin to loosen the knot by pulling at the thoughts behind it, until you uncover the real reason, the root cause, inside yourself. Even if you uncover more than one reason for your feelings, you should—after about five *why* questions—gain deeper insight about what's causing your actions or reactions.

- "Unravel a knot" by writing out the Five Whys in your Personal Log or on the pages provided here (see pages 90 and 91).

Before you start, take a few moments to review the following samples of the Five Whys practice.

SAMPLE APPLICATION—UNRAVELING A KNOT OF ANGER

A coworker and I worked late several nights and over a weekend to meet a deadline that a project manager moved up, calling it "urgent." I had to miss my nephew's birthday party in order to get it done. On Monday morning, we found out that the deadline had changed again, and even though there had been plenty of time to inform us of this change, the project manager hadn't told us. His reasoning was that ". . . it needed to be done anyway, and this way we were sure to meet the deadline." I was furious.

Here are five *why* questions she might ask herself to uncover the root of her reaction:

1. Why am I so furious about the way the project manager acted? Because he was out of line—inconsiderate, demanding, and unreasonable.

2. *Why do I think he was unreasonable?*
Because he knew we didn't have to push that hard and didn't bother to tell us. He disregarded the fact that I have a life outside work. He obviously doesn't respect me.

3. *Why do I think he doesn't respect me?*
Because if he did, he would have told us we had another couple of days to finish the work, and I wouldn't have missed a family event that was important to me. I'm willing to work long hours and make sacrifices, because doing a good job is important, but I don't want him to take advantage of me, which is what he did.

4. *Why do I think he takes advantage of me?*
Well, he is a hard-driving manager, but I'm the one who didn't speak up in this case. At other times, now that I think about it, he has renegotiated deadlines if he can, or gotten some additional resources patched in to help. He's also gone out of his way to say thank you for the extra effort.

5. *Why didn't I speak up this time?*
Because I didn't want to look uncommitted or risk letting other people down. I don't want to be seen as lazy.

Insight: I'm taking out some of my anger at myself for not speaking up. Maybe next time I can cut him a little more slack—trust him more—and try speaking up when I need some support or when the deadlines seem unreasonable.

SAMPLE APPLICATION—UNRAVELING A KNOT OF
CRAVING

> *When he finally got around to cleaning out his garage
> before a move, he found—among the rakes, tools, and oil
> cans—about nine sets of golf clubs.* Well, *he reasoned,*
> we have been in this house for a long time. Stuff
> does sort of pile up. *Golf is not an easy game, and just
> cutting down a few strokes can make a big difference.
> You've got to keep up with the latest in golf technology—
> titanium clubheads, newer and better shafts, more accu-
> rate putters—if you expect any respect out on the links.
> Later, sitting down to read one of the two golf magazines
> he subscribed to, he wondered,* Did all those clubs
> really improve my game that much?

Here are five *why* questions he might ask himself to
uncover the root of his reaction:

1. *Why do I want all these sets of clubs?*
Well, last year I just wasn't getting the distance on my
drives. The clubs I was using were costing me twenty
to thirty yards on every hole.

2. *Why is it so important to get more distance on my drives?*
In the end, golf is a game of inches. You know, every
stroke counts, and I'll take every advantage I can get.

3. *Why do I need to take every advantage I can get?*
A guy I golf with got a new set of clubs this year, and
his handicap has already dropped by three strokes. I
used to beat him almost all the time. Now we're just
about even—in fact, I think his handicap is lower
than mine.

4. *Why is it important that we be so competitive?*
We always have a bet going . . . but it's not the money, really. I just hate losing.

5. *Why is losing or winning so important?*
To be honest, it really hurts my pride. I don't want to be looked at as a loser. When you lose, it's like not being a part of the club or something. I hate second best.

Insight: What other, more lasting areas of my life can fulfill that core desire for me? Is that desire really meaningful in the long run? Yeah, I guess when I throw a baseball around with my kids, I get a great sense of satisfaction. Winning doesn't really enter into it. They just love it when I play with them. They don't seem to care about the ball slipping through the torn pocket of the glove I've had since . . .

SAMPLE APPLICATION—UNRAVELING A KNOT OF CRAVING

They've gone out three times and she's more than just "interested" in him. In fact, she finds it hard to concentrate; fantasizing about him distracts her at work as well as at home. Any misgivings about his potential bad qualities are ignored; she exaggerates his charming, sensitive, and successful side, telling herself, I've finally met Mr. Right, *and secretly wishing he called every night instead of twice a week. She hasn't contacted her friends lately, not wanting to miss any opportunities to see him. When she does venture out of her apartment, she shops for new clothes and spends money she doesn't really have so she can always look her best for him.*

Here are five *why* questions she might ask herself to uncover the root of her reaction:

1. Why am I having such trouble concentrating at work?
Because I'm really happy about meeting Mr. Right and I'm thinking about him a lot, how wonderful it will be when we're together, happily married . . .

2. Why is being with Mr. Right so important to me?
Because he's so wonderful—everything I want in a man. This relationship just has to work. I couldn't stand it if this one doesn't last.

3. Why is having this relationship work out so important to me?
Because I'm tired of feeling lonely and unfulfilled. I can't stand another night at home, by myself, with the television for company. I need someone in my life, a romantic partner, to be happy.

4. Why do I need a romantic partner to be happy?
Because I often feel empty, restless, and afraid to be alone, and I think being with him will take care of all that.

5. Why do I feel lonely and unfulfilled?
I don't know. Maybe I'm just not happy with myself. My life feels so unsettled, like I'm spinning my wheels. And in addition to that, I don't have anyone with whom to share it.

Insight: I will still need to understand and appreciate myself better even if I am in a relationship. If this relationship does work out, we will probably have conflict and difficult times. Every good relationship has conflict. I'll have to be comfortable with my own life to make this work.

SAMPLE APPLICATION—UNRAVELING A KNOT OF
DELUSION

> *In the early years of their marriage, she would half joke about his perfectionism, but her words had no meaning for him. The kidding turned into constant squabbles about household duties, money, and sex. Almost nothing was "good enough," but he didn't take her seriously when she continually asked him to stop being so critical and impatient with her. He would often dismiss her comments and suggestions as if they were her problem—as if she was just blowing things out of proportion. Then a performance report, completed by his employees, echoed his wife's years of complaints. After an incident with a coworker, he realized that denying his hypercritical nature had probably cost him a promotion he really wanted.*

Here are five *why* questions he might ask himself to uncover the root of his reaction:

1. *Why didn't I pay attention to my wife's feedback?*
   Because I've always seen her as too needy and demanding. She expects too much from me.

2. *Why have I seen her in that light?*
   Because she has often wanted more attention than I've been willing to give her.

3. *Why have I been unwilling to give her the attention she wants?*
   Because I've often felt inadequate when she asks for more . . . and I hate that feeling.

4. *Why do I feel inadequate?*
   Because I rarely saw the kind of exchange she's asking for between my parents, and I'm not sure I can do it . . . I don't think I know how.

5. *Why am I unsure that I can do what she is asking for?*
Because it is really scary to be emotionally intimate . . . I feel too vulnerable.

Insight: I realize that I am afraid of feeling deep emotion
for a variety of reasons—undemonstrative parents,
missed opportunities, old rejections. I guess I have been
carrying on this way, sort of not paying attention to her
feelings, or mine, for quite some time. It seems comfortable in some ways, yet I know that something is wrong.

UNRAVELING MENTAL KNOTS

1. *Why* _____

_____

_____

_____

2. *Why* _____

_____

_____

_____

3. *Why* _____

_____

_____

_____

4. *Why* _____

_____

_____

_____

5. Why _____

_____

_____

_____

Insight: _____

_____

_____

_____

_____

_____

_____

_____

_____

_____

_____

_____

_____

_____

_____

_____

_____

_____

_____

WORKING WITH MENTAL PROJECTIONS

> If you look in a mirror, it's most important to realize
> that what you see is not at all solid.
>
> AKONG TULKU RINPOCHE[14]

Just as reality projects itself onto a mirror, we project
our moods, motives, or flaws onto the faces of others.
We see faults in public figures, family members, and
coworkers but deny them in ourselves. The same could
be said of taking our "good" qualities and the qualities
of those we love for granted. What we don't see in ourselves we notice in others. We tend to react strongly to
those aspects of others that we don't like—or don't
know—about ourselves.

I still remember the comment an executive made in
one of our emotional intelligence seminars. We had
just shown a quick series of twenty faces and asked the
participants to identify the feeling in each one. At first
glance, the task appeared elementary, but due to the
subtleties in the facial expressions it required consider-
able concentration to answer correctly.

At the end of the activity, she said, "I missed a lot
more than I expected. I marked many of the people
angry, and I was wrong . . . maybe *I am the one who is
angry!*"

When we are unaware of our projections, it causes
difficulties in our relationships at home and at work.
The following practice helps us see the fluid nature of
the "objects of our mind"—our projections and perceptions. Once aware, our mental formations can be
exposed for what they really are—"smoke in the
mirror."

PRACTICES

SEEING THE SMOKE IN THE MIRROR

This practice is a visualization exercise taught by Akong Tulku Rinpoche at the Kagyu Samyé Ling Tibetan Center in Scotland. Smoke in the Mirror teaches us that we can transmute our mental formations, letting go of the ones that are "poison" and keeping those that serve us well. The exercise asks you to create your reflection in an imaginary mirror (or, if you prefer, you can use a real mirror) in order to become aware of your projections, let go of the ones that cloud your view and limit your potential, and keep the ones that help you.

WHAT YOU'LL NEED

- About fifteen minutes at the end of your day for about two weeks.

- A quiet, private place.

- Your Personal Log.

TRY THIS

- Take the first five minutes to breathe mindfully. Feel your breath come in and go out, in and out. Keep full awareness on the in-breath, full awareness on the out-breath . . . then start the practice.

- Imagine a mirror out in front of you. While breathing in, out, in and out, notice your emotions, thoughts, and sensations. After a few minutes, when your mind settles, look at your reflection in the mirror, making an effort to notice both the negative and positive thoughts and feelings that go through your mind.

- Focusing on your exhalation, breathe all feelings and sensations into the reflection. Whether you are sad, furious, satisfied, or happy, let each one of them go, expelling them into the mirror. Gently and slowly, release them with your out-breath. Do the same with your thoughts, and then again with the tension spots in your body.

- As you breathe out, notice that you are emptying yourself, letting go of all the feelings, thoughts, sensations—moving them gradually, one at a time, into the mirror. Continue this breathing and letting go for three or four minutes.

- Once you have emptied your thoughts, feelings, and sensations, let your mind settle. Then begin to study the reflection. At first, just look at the image of yourself portrayed in the imaginary mirror, noticing all the different attributes—those you consider "good" and those you consider "bad."

- Notice any judgments you hold about yourself, the thoughts, and the feelings that arise when you look in the mirror. Observe their fluid, ever-changing nature—as if they were billows of smoke taking shape, then dissipating into nothing. Linger, absorbing this notion, breathing in, breathing out.

- Be aware that what you see are the ideas and mental formations you carry about yourself, projections— frail wispy figments of smoke. Then, with each in-breath, take in the qualities you desire, bringing them back into yourself. Leave the rest in the mirror.

- Continue breathing deeply in this way for several minutes. Notice how you can choose what you take in, that you can cultivate the positive qualities and mental attitudes you have recognized.

- Complete the practice by taking one or two minutes to relax the mind, letting thoughts come and go with an easy flow.

- After the exercise, take a few minutes to write and reflect on the following questions:

Which qualities did I choose to breathe back into myself?

_____

_____

_____

Which qualities did I leave in the mirror?

_____

_____

_____

What was it like to see them go up in smoke—to realize they are merely formations in my mind—not solid?

_____

_____

_____

What ideas about myself—such as self-imposed limitations or long-held views—do I want to change?

_____

_____

_____

_____

Continue doing this exercise for at least one week or until it becomes quite easy to project feelings into the mirror. It is important to do this practice in short sessions only—about ten minutes once a day. At least two or three minutes of relaxation should precede and follow each session. Do not continue if you experience strong fear or have other intense reactions—move on to the practices for cultivating calm in the next chapter and come back to this practice at a later time.

VISUALIZING A POSITIVE MODEL

Although this variation draws upon centuries-old Tibetan practices in meditation, it is similar to methods used by modern-day Olympians, professional athletes, and performing artists. This type of visualization is used to break self-defeating thoughts, release performance anxieties, and learn new skills. By doing this practice consistently, new neural pathways are formed in our brains. I studied visualization techniques in my training as a psychologist, used them personally to overcome a fear of public speaking, and have found they accelerate progress for many of my clients.

WHAT YOU'LL NEED

- About twenty minutes of undisturbed time.

- A quiet, private place to sit or lie down.

- Your Personal Log.

TRY THIS

- Begin the exercise by thinking of a person who has an emotional habit you would like to emulate (some examples include: maintaining your dignity when being talked down to, calmly asserting yourself when you are afraid, or staying open to feedback when criticized). If no one individual comes to mind, create a composite image, drawing from a number of people you admire.

- After you've decided on an "ideal" model, project an image of that model in an imaginary mirror.

- Go inside his viewpoint, attitude, or mind-set. Experience how it feels to be him: unafraid, willing to risk, hopeful in the face of a setback, generous, forgiving.

- When you feel you've experienced his viewpoint, attitude, or mind-set as fully as possible, return to yourself. Spend one to two minutes breathing mindfully; on the out-breath, breathe out your misgivings, fear, anger, and craving. On the in-breath, breathe in positive qualities and mind-sets.

- Write down what you learned about the antidote to your mental knot, noting shifts in your perspective. Consider what you could do to foster these more positive mental formations in yourself, and write down

one or two ideas about what you can do to build this
emotional habit going forward.

TRAIL MARKER

Stop here for a moment and look back at the trail that
led you through self-awareness. Following the ancient
map of the Establishments of Mindfulness, you have vis-
ited the telltale signs of stress carried by the body and
recognized the warning signs they carry of an
impending amygdala hijack. You have dipped downward to touch the emotions behind those physical
signs, the patterns and habits of response, and—farther
down—their root causes. With new clarity, you are
ready to determine where you want to go from here
and what new emotional habits you want to shape along
the way.

Although you may have felt impatient to move
through the valley of self, you can find comfort in
knowing that a finely tuned awareness is necessary to
reach the elevations of serenity and harmony. Shortcuts
on the road to personal transformation lead to only
passing changes. Your hard-won self-knowledge lays the
groundwork for retooling your neuropathways,
opening new roads, new choices.

Before going on, take a moment to clarify your direction.

What emotional habits would I like to change in my life? Why?

_____

_____

_____

_____

What barriers to personal change have I uncovered?

_____

_____

_____

_____

What strengths in myself would I like to build on?

_____

_____

_____

_____

From here your path turns upward toward a higher place of joy and compassion, out of the valley to a summit of stillness, a point of poise: the capacity to *manage* the habits and patterns you have now uncovered.

CHAPTER 7

STAYING POISED

Grace under pressure.

ERNEST HEMINGWAY

Pause for a moment. Consider the complexity of the feelings, thoughts, and actions that result from trillions of neural connections in your brain. Consider, too, your power to form and re-form those connections, guiding your brain's further development. Knowing how the pathways in your brain create the experiences of your life—and how, in turn, your actions and thoughts construct those pathways—you are now ready to set a new course toward conscious change.

We are in that pivotal moment where we actually begin to reshape our emotional habits. At this point in our efforts, we reconstruct our brains, physically change the patterns of our minds, and participate in our own evolution as individuals and as a species. But the process of developing poise happens over time. Old habits die hard.

It was a familiar pattern: taking on too much and over-committing. This time, she could even see what was happening, but it didn't change the fact that there were still project deadlines, e-mails to answer, phone calls to return, and kids to take care of . . . all waiting for her. After cut-

backs at the office, she was now doing the work of three people. The load was overwhelming. Her mind spun, flooded by stress—she was having trouble thinking clearly.

In the past, when she was in a panicked state, she had missed deadlines, gone to meetings unprepared, and turned in poor-quality work. She worried she would let people down, again. I can't manage it all! *she thought. She tried to tell her boyfriend about the pressure she felt and how she couldn't stay focused or get herself organized. Touchy and ill at ease, she argued with him when he "didn't get it."* "Just forget it," *she said and slammed the phone down.*

Then she caught herself in the midst of the tailspin and stopped. Wait a minute, what's going on here? *she asked herself.* Is it *true* that I can't manage it all? *She slowed down, breathed deeply, and sat in meditation. After regaining a sense of calm, she wrote down all the things that she had to get done in the next several weeks. Her mind clear, she got out her calendar and made a plan to manage her time.*

With a sigh of relief, she thought, Thankfully, I got myself back on track and didn't go off the deep end. Now about that matter of calling my boyfriend to apologize . . .

To calm the amygdala and prevent the brain from triggering again and again, we need to *be still.* At a minimum, this requires a ten- to fifteen-second *pause* that allows the thinking brain to re-engage. By taking a few brief moments to cool off and soothe ourselves, we arrest the flow of stress hormones surging through the body. We are now free to choose an alternative route, a new and better way of responding.

Beyond the initial short-circuiting, we need to manage
the aftereffects of the amygdala hijack: Stress hormones
not only douse us in the moment, but also stay in our
system for hours, even days afterward. This hormone-
induced state keeps the brain ready for action and
primed to react again—a hair trigger set to respond to
even the smallest of provocations. We may feel edgy, agitated, and overly critical. At these times, the challenge is
to consistently pause, to develop a *habit* of poise.

As outlined in chapter 2, The Science of Emotions,
when we encounter a real or symbolic threat, the amygdala signals its alert, mobilizing an instant response by
activating our survival mechanisms, physically and psy-
chologically. We react, our neurons firing down the old,
well-worn neural pathways, hijacking our powers of reasoned thinking. Once the emotional brain takes over,
our "ability to hear, think, and speak with clarity dis-
solves,"[1] leaving us at the mercy of our least sophisticated
habits—banging the phone, freezing in fear, or cringing
in shame. And each time we react out of our old habits,
we reinforce them. We travel down the same path,
etching it more deeply with each stressful encounter.

Staying poised suspends this automatic reaction.
Instead of well-worn, knee-jerk responses, stronger
habits of poise grant us quicker access to the thinking
brain. The temptation to attack and argue may still flit
through our mind—a momentary impulse—but now
we can let it pass through our mind and out again.

At first, the moment of poise may take place in the
seconds just after an amygdala hijack—a sign that we
are becoming more aware. But the power to short-
circuit the attack *before* we act is the true goal. Developing this skill "demands a . . . profound change at the
neurological level: both weakening the existing habit

and replacing it with a better one."[2] Staying poised is, in part, the decisive pause that begins the process of retooling our circuitry. It opens a new fork in the old road, allowing us to choose a different route.

When we are triggered and retriggered and retriggered once again—as in the story of the overwhelmed and pressured woman at the beginning of this chapter—the body floods, the mind jams. We become paralyzed and need a "time-out" to interrupt swirling thoughts and feelings. If we wait out the surge of stress hormones, we can calm ourselves and apply our mind to prioritizing tasks.

Or, if fear has been activated, we may feel the urge to run away from a conflict or situation that needs our attention. Thoughts like, *It's too hard; I'm not up to it; If I say something it will only make things worse,* circle through our mind. We want to escape, avoid the difficulty. Rather than withdrawing in shaken silence, we can build an inner refuge—a safe place to challenge our fear-ridden thoughts and gather our resources to face the situation at hand.

Sometimes, when we are frightened, anger can rise as a defense. We may be tempted to strike back with a caustic counterattack. Too often, this impulse fuels the fire and escalates a conflict. Instead, we need to cool down, formulate our thoughts, and engage in a forthright, honest dialogue.

To build these alternative habits, we need a repertoire of skills that can be called upon when we need it most. Alleviating the effect of an amygdala hijack requires us to draw on a number of calming methods that work in different ways and at various times during, after, and even before the stressful event.

The first is an immediate, "in the moment" response, which consists of both *recognizing* an amygdala hijack and *waiting out* the limbic surge. The simple thought, *I'm having an amygdala hijack,* in and of itself activates the thinking brain, short-circuiting the hijack. But we still need methods to counteract the initial burst of catecholamine, the stress hormone that generates a quick rush of energy for a vigorous fight or flight, saturating the body for several minutes after an amygdala hijack.

To calm yourself in these moments, there are a number of things you can do, such as touch an acupressure point, count to ten, take a hot bath, work out at the gym, or go for a long walk. Physical relaxation methods of this kind rapidly shift the body into a lower arousal state, quelling agitated thoughts. Sometimes, however, these methods are impractical—you can't get away from the situation or change your environment. You're stuck.

In all circumstances, though, you have to breathe, so you can use this to your advantage. Taking long breaths instead of the shallow, rapid breathing common to stress has a direct, positive effect on both body and mind. Breathe in. Breathe out. Fully, deeply. Do this for at least fifteen seconds or about five long breaths. Mindful breathing was introduced in chapter 3, Tuning In, as an awareness technique. Now you apply this same skill during moments of acute stress, creating a temporary pause to allow the surge of catecholamine to pass. Hold steady—aware of your body, doing nothing, saying little—until your mind clears.

What you do in these moments is vital to changing your emotional habits. So are the hours that follow. In addition to the first surge of catecholamine, the amygdala's "emergency alarm" sets off ripples of adrenaline and cortisol through the body. This "stew of stress hormones secreted when a person is upset takes hours to become reabsorbed in the body and fade away."[3] In fact, it takes at least four to six hours and sometimes several days. The resulting state of heightened arousal causes us to become touchy, quick-tempered, moody—vulnerable not only to conflicts in the world "out there," but also to the discord within our own mind. We can easily be triggered by recycling negative thoughts, knots of worry, resentment, or spite—the poisons of the mind. This is more than just a metaphor. When our own toxic thoughts trigger the amygdala, we quite literally poison the mind with stress hormones.

Counteracting the extended aftermath of an amygdala hijack—the "red zone" of hormonal arousal—makes up the second key aspect of staying poised. By turning to practices that strengthen composure, we can develop the ability to soothe our distress and ease our inflamed thoughts for longer periods of time. Some of the most powerful techniques come from the Eastern traditions of meditation and visualization, and several are introduced in the practices that follow.

However, wresting control of our emotions does not mean eradicating or running away from them. We cannot "wish" our way out of how we feel, but we can—with effort—learn grace under pressure. According to Robert Ornstein, president of the Institute for the Study of Human Knowledge and a professor at Stanford, "People can consciously redirect their minds, but, like learning to read or do math, this ability doesn't come naturally. It has to be nurtured."[4] With the right effort, you *will* be able to increase your ability to remain calm in the face of stress. With sustained practice—in the moment, hours after a hijack, and before a confrontation develops—you will also reduce the amount of time it takes to achieve a state of calm.

A few years back, I worked with a major-league baseball player getting ready for the American League playoffs. He was having difficulty hitting a particular pitcher on the opposing team. In fact, he had never been successful against him. I suggested deep breathing, focused relaxation, and a visualization activity. His challenge was to develop a metaphor that would mirror his actions when he stepped up to the plate. He chose the egret, a large shorebird that either stands still or tiptoes along the water's edge while stalking its prey, then strikes with the split-second force of lightning. He wanted to maintain this patient, measured calm until his bat attacked the pitch.

We started with short sessions, then gradually increased the periods of relaxation and visualization. Already an incredibly focused professional, he took to the "thought training" easily. After weeks of progressive practice, he was able to "flash" on the image of the egret—his mental cue—and instantly move into the groove of focused, alert relaxation. His achievements (two home runs against his feared adversary, a Most Valuable Player award, and, later, a World Series ring) provide an excellent example of the time, effort, and *process* required to fully make use of these methods. Like hitting a difficult pitch, the time you spend learning to soothe afflictive emotions *before* a moment of confrontation will greatly improve your chances of success.

Researchers at the University of Pittsburgh and

Carnegie Mellon University have shown that as people
mentally prepare for a given challenge, they activate
the prefrontal cortex—the executive center of the
brain that can shut down an amygdala hijack. In fact,
"the prefrontal cortex becomes *particularly active* when
a person has to prepare to overcome a *habitual*
response" (italics mine).[5] Without this engagement
of the prefrontal lobe, we are more likely to use the
"old route," acting out our ingrained, undesirable
habits.

Conditioning your response through visualization—a
form of mental rehearsal—accelerates your progress.
With extended practice, you will be able to flash on a
symbol or a personal cue to lower your physical arousal
and ease your distressed emotions. You can signal your
neural impulses to travel an alternative route, making a
conscious choice to react differently. Which leads to the
third key aspect of staying poised.

Although practicing poise in both the seconds and
hours after a hijacking is a vital step toward rewiring the
brain, the long-term goal is *proactive* poise. What we
seek is a ready state of resolute calm. For this, we need
to exercise and build up the left prefrontal area of the
brain—the center of upbeat and optimistic feelings—so
that the *inhibitory* neurons can more easily contain the
firing of *excitatory* neurons during an amygdala hijack.
Cliff Saron, a psychologist at Albert Einstein Medical
School in New York City, reports that "those individuals
with more left-sided frontal activation may be better at
turning off their amygdalas once they get activated so
that negative emotions do not linger."[6] As we saw in the
study of scientists at Promega back in chapter 2, practicing mindful meditation on a daily basis develops the
left prefrontal lobe. With this part of the brain acti-

vated, not only can we recover more quickly from amygdala hijacks, but we are less vulnerable to them altogether.

When working to develop poise, remember that the process is not easy. You are reversing "decades of learning that resides in heavily traveled, highly reinforced neural circuitry, built up over years of repeating [your old] habit."[7] You may feel that one step forward is followed by two steps back. After all, you are putting the relatively young neocortex to work in a job long held by parts of the brain that adapted to a world very different from our own. Deep and lasting change takes time and determined practice, and each of these methods will help you develop some aspect of the grace under pressure that is poise.

Portia Nelson's poem "Autobiography in Five Chapters"[8] captures this process of change:

CHAPTER ONE

I walk down the street.
> There is a deep hole in the sidewalk.
> I fall in.
> I am lost. . . . I am helpless.
>> It isn't my fault.
It takes forever to find a way out.

CHAPTER TWO

I walk down the same street.
> There is a deep hole in the sidewalk.
> I pretend I don't see it.
> I fall in again.
I can't believe I'm in the same place.
>> But, it isn't my fault.
It still takes a long time to get out.

CHAPTER THREE

I walk down the same street.
>There is a deep hole in the sidewalk.
>I *see* it is there.
>I still fall in . . . it's a habit . . . but,
>>my eyes are open.
>>I know where I am.

It is *my* fault.
I get out immediately.

CHAPTER FOUR

I walk down the same street.
>There is a deep hole in the sidewalk.
>I walk around it.

CHAPTER FIVE

I walk down another street.

Do not be discouraged if, after a short while, you see little change in yourself. Breaking trail can be hard work, and some missteps and falling back into old habits are normal. Developing neuropathways takes persistence and, at first, conscious effort. Over time, new avenues will open.

QUIETING FEAR

When the amygdala reads a symbolic event as threatening, it mobilizes the body "to respond with a strong emotion, *particularly fear.*"[9] In order to reestablish poise in the minutes, hours, and days that follow an amygdala hijack, it is important to allay the potent, disorienting, and disabling emotion of fear. To counteract fear's unsettling effects, visualizing a circle of protection around ourselves can be a powerful technique.

Many teachers in the East advise that we hold a circle of protection around ourselves *at all times,* while awake and during sleep, to guard ourselves from unexpected agitation or danger. Although most effective when used *before* going into a situation that could trigger you, this practice can also be applied immediately *after* an amygdala hijack. Either way, we calm down more quickly and think clearly again, seeing choices we may have missed in our agitated state. No longer riddled with fear, we can make choices true to our integrity, less apt to react with knee-jerk aggression or passive withdrawal.

Used in religious traditions around the world, the circle represents wholeness. It is often referred to as a mandala (meaning "to surround with beauty"). In the Tibetan tradition, for example, the custom of painting a mandala with rings of fire is said to fend off harm. In the West, we may sprinkle holy water, pray the rosary, or invoke warrior angels to keep us safe. Indigenous cultures often place stones in a circle or circumambulate a consecrated space with a smudge stick of incense or myrrh.

We can also tap into the unconscious mind—in a less physical, more figurative way—through the use of imagery. This practice evokes personal qualities that give us strength and clarity. For instance, we may imagine a circle around ourselves to symbolize our psychological space, our sacred heart-mind that no outsider can invade or control. By doing this, we create a safe haven within, a sovereignty and responsibility for our own decisions and choices.

This particular version of the Circle of Protection was extracted by Dosho Port-sensei from *The Blue Cliff*

Record, a thirteenth-century collection of one hundred anecdotes from Chinese Ch'an teachers.[10] Its source is koan number 18,[11] named for the place it was written, the Blue Cliff in the Hunan province of China. I have broadened Port-sensei's practice, using a general archetype or "wisdom figure" to represent the desired attribute rather than a specific Eastern entity.

In this practice, we begin by imagining ourselves standing or sitting on a floor of cobalt blue. The deep blue color represents the energy of healing in Eastern Tantric[12] traditions, as well as representing a soothing quality. It is believed to help us enter into "stability" or "stillness" in meditation.

Next, drawing directly from the ancient text, we visualize ourselves surrounded by a breathing sphere of pearls and agates, translucent and impermeable. The deep red color of agates is said to reduce fear, foster initiative, and enrich courage, while the milky white, opalescent pearl represents unity, grace, and glory. Visualizing the sphere of agates and pearls suggests the importance and precious dignity of each individual's being—something to protect and cherish.

We go on to imagine four wisdom figures—one in front, one in back, one to the left, and one to the right—guarding this sacred place. Each represents a specific quality that inspires us, guides us, and helps us resolve the dilemmas we face. Within the pearly sphere of safety and acceptance, the purpose of meditating on these figures is to draw out their qualities in ourselves, calling forth our inner wisdom, empowering us to act on our own behalf or on behalf of others.

This meditation creates a circle of protection, an inviolable refuge within that we must hold sacred. Teachers in the East advise us *never* to relinquish our circle of protection, our ultimate responsibility for ourselves, to *any* external force—be it a lover, fame and fortune, a commanding leader, or even a venerated spiritual teacher.

PRACTICE

CREATING A CIRCLE OF PROTECTION

Although this practice describes the general attributes of four wisdom figures (wisdom, compassion, action, and empowerment), it will be more meaningful if you include specific figures from your own cultural or spiritual background. Virtually all traditions, in some way, draw on the power of the four archetypes presented here.[13] The guardian figures may be holy people or saints from history, representations of the divine, ancestors or loved ones from your own life, or a patchwork of attributes from several people you admire. (See the appendix, Examples of Wisdom Figures from a Variety of Religious Traditions and Modern Culture, for archetypes you might use in this meditation.)

Although some people are concerned that they "cannot visualize," in reality imagery may be experienced in many different ways. The range includes seeing a mental picture; hearing the wind blow or the echo of the voice of a loved one; smelling a sweet fragrance; or intuiting the sense of an idea.[14] Since there is no wrong way to use imagery, any or all of these approaches work. Most people succeed if they follow their natural tendencies and style.

Working with the Circle of Protection meditation

will sharpen your visualization skills, bringing the images to life. After you repeat the practice many times, it takes root in your unconscious pathways. With extended practice, you will be able to "flash" on the circle of protection in a moment of stress—calling it to mind vividly and quickly—and feel its effects within moments.

WHAT YOU'LL NEED

- About fifteen minutes at the beginning or end of your day.

- A quiet, private place.

- Your Personal Log.

TRY THIS

- Take at least five minutes to relax: Sit comfortably with your spine upright. Do several minutes of deep breathing: Focus on your breathing. Feel it come in and go out, in and out. Ride the waves of your own breath. Keep full awareness on the in-breath, full awareness on the out-breath. Let the breath just happen, observing it wherever and however you feel it—a rise and fall of your belly, a coolness in your nose, a pressure in your lungs.

- As you breathe in, say to yourself, *Breathing in, I know I am breathing in.* And as you breathe out, say, *Breathing out, I know I am breathing out.* Just that. You recognize your in-breath as an in-breath and your out-breath as an out-breath. As your relaxation deepens, let your mind echo *In* and *Out* with the rhythm of your breath.

- Begin the practice by imaging yourself standing or sitting on a floor of cobalt blue. Deep, rich, soothing blue holding you up, supporting you.

- Visualize a sphere surrounding you—at a comfortable distance out in front and around you—with walls and a ceiling of pearls and agates, translucent and impermeable.

- Behind you, picture a guardian of Wisdom, the figure of discriminating insight. He is noble, gentle, and often carries a sword to symbolize his mental clarity and penetrating insight. With flashing awareness, he cuts through delusion and sees into the deeper essence of every situation. Imagine he is cutting through anything other than the Truth.

- In front of you is a figure of Compassion. She is endless mercy, "the one who hears the cries of the world." She embodies the gentle, responsive, and empathic qualities of compassion and the perfection of generosity. Her quality is fluid—taking many different forms, each appropriate to the situation. She sometimes holds a rosary, blue lotus flower, or glass of nectar in her hands and can be acknowledged by the presence of a sweet smell. She asks that we pay attention to what has heart and meaning.

- To your left is the bodhisattva[15] of Action. She carries a wish-fulfilling gem. She personifies love in action, virtue, diligent training, and patience. Imbued with clear intention and dignity, she acts calmly and with deliberation. In order to do good work and inspire others, she often works secretly, anonymously, helping those who are suffering. An expression of wisdom and ethical conduct in the real world, she sees the interconnection of the universe, solves problems systemically, and guards and cares for all.

- To the right is a figure of Empowerment. He brings people knowledge of the necessity of liberation. Possessing great authority and enlightened power, he impels us to carry our voice and creativity into the world, at home, at work, and in the larger society. Symbolizing wisdom in action, he has the power to break the bonds of those who are suffering, to offer them freedom from patterns of denial and indulgence.

- With each breath, absorb the safety of being in the presence of these guardians. Breathe in wisdom, breathe out fear. Breathe in compassion, breathe out danger. Breathe in clarity about how to act and react to the situation you face, breathe out confusion. Breathe in the power of your voice, the intrinsic dignity of your existence. Breathe out fear. With each breath, absorb calm strength.

- Take a moment to look at the issue before you—the cause of your distress—from the perspective of each of these wisdom figures.

  ~ *How does the guardian of wisdom look at this situation? What do I see when I "cut through" the fears I hold about what I face?*

  ~ Allow yourself to be held in tender compassion. *What thoughts or beliefs are triggering my reaction?* Look at the other person(s) through the eyes of your compassion figure. *What do you see?*

~ Visit the perspective of the bodhisattva of action (as if you are putting her mind-set on over your mind-set, like a woolen cap). *What action is called for in this situation? What is the most ethical response?*

~ *What qualities will empower me to act effectively in this situation?* Let the figure of empowerment give you counsel, perhaps letting him give you a symbol of the strength you desire.

• Linger, staying in this meditation for at least fifteen to twenty minutes. When you are finished, gently return your attention to your routine, refreshed and ready to return to your day-to-day responsibilities, carrying your sense of safety and circle of protection with you wherever you go.

You may want to take a moment to note key insights from this meditation in your Personal Log.

_____

_____

_____

_____

EASING THE MIND

Another aspect of reestablishing poise is soothing the mind. In the hormone-saturated state that follows an amygdala hijack, we are more vulnerable to emotionally driven thoughts—anger, jealousy, or spite. Easily preoccupied or distracted by craving and discontent, we nurse old wounds, revisit what we "should have" said, and brood over unfulfilled desires. Thoughts of this kind are mini triggers for the amygdala, releasing yet more stress hormones into the body and further skewing our already off-kilter mind toward negativity. Just as we need to quiet our fear and cool our anger in the aftermath of an amygdala hijack, we must also guard our mind in the hours and days that follow.

Here, too, we can use visualization to quiet ourselves and reroute our thinking. Based on their review of contemporary research, Errol Korn and Karen Johnson, in *Visualization: The Uses of Imagery in the Health Professions,* say, "Imagery provides the quickest and surest way of programming the body." They conclude, "The use of the images is a more complete and rapid means of entering the [brain's] frequency domain, where the brain actually works."[16]

Although modern research now supports its efficacy, visualization is a technique long known to the ancient Hindu, Chinese, and shamanic healers. It appears in some of the oldest teachings known, including the literature of Tantric traditions and cabalism (Hebrew mysticism). For instance, Ayurvedic medicine, originating in the Vedic traditions of India and practiced for more than three thousand years, uses visualization and imagery as part of its approach to healing illness. Believing that body, mind, and spirit are intimately connected, Ayurveda prescribes visualizations to soothe the mind and stop negative thoughts associated with "disease."

The following practice—drawn from Ayurvedic and Tantric beliefs about color imagery and strongly supported by modern Western psychology—uses a deep, indigo blue-black color to ease the "venom" of angry thoughts. Consider a doctor's or dentist's waiting room painted in vibrant red or orange. It can make the wait seem never-ending, while a blue or green waiting room will do the opposite. So, too, imaging a particular color of light can mitigate our dour mood or brighten the gloomiest amygdala-ridden day.

Other colors suggested for easing jealousy, discontent, delusion, and craving are noted at the end of the practice.[17] I learned these techniques in my studies with Khenchen Thrangu Rinpoche[18] at his monastery in Kathmandu, Nepal, near the Great Boudanath Stupa.

There are several important things to keep in mind when using this practice:

- Imagine the colored lights as having a soothing quality that assuages raw emotions and eases negative thinking. The lights are a symbol of the healing potential of our own minds, and over time facility and confidence in using this meditation will grow. With practice, the colors become easier and easier to visualize and help us feel increasingly relaxed.

- Visualize the colored light entering the body with the in-breath, and the negative emotion as being expelled with the out-breath. Imagine the light permeating the heart, mind, *and* body, since Tantric tradition holds that these three sources of life are deeply intertwined.

- Remember that each mental knot is not separate and discrete from the others. For example, there can be angry discontent, jealous discontent, craving rooted in discontent, and so on. Even though we are focusing on one color at a time, beginning with blue-black to ease anger and hatred, each color can benefit all the other mental knots.

With time and extended practice, you will be agile enough to flash on a particular color, using this cue to release agitated thoughts. But first, it is best to master the method by using the longer application that follows here.

P R A C T I C E

 VISUALIZING BLUE-BLACK LIGHT TO COUNTERACT ANGER[19]

WHAT YOU'LL NEED

- Thirty minutes to complete the practice.

- A quiet place to sit or lie down. If sitting, use a straight-backed chair or sit on a cushion on the floor so that your body is relaxed and your spine is erect. If you lie down, make sure you're in a comfortable position where you can breathe easily and keep an alert mind.

- Your Personal Log.

TRY THIS

- Begin this meditation with five minutes of mindful breathing. Feel the space around you, where you are, and become aware of the sensations of the body as it is resting on the ground. Notice the breath moving in and out . . . in and out, effortlessly. Then start the practice.

- Look at the feelings of anger and hatred in your mind. Consider their harmful consequences in your day-to-day life—both the physical and the emotional effects—by thinking about the following questions:

  ~ *Where in my body do I hold anger or hatred?* (If you have any trouble identifying where you hold these emotions in your body, use the body tension scan from chapter 3 to raise your awareness.)

  ~ *When I am angry, what fantasies of "getting even" pass through my mind?*

  ~ *How do these thoughts color my mood and affect the way I see other situations?*

  ~ *How do I typically act when I'm angry?*

  ~ *What is the effect of my anger on others around me?*

- Imagine a clear blue sky pasted with white puffy clouds or a black velvet sky hanging with diamond stars. From afar, a sphere of colored lights made up of jewel-like white, green, yellow, sky-blue, red, and deep blue colors appears. These lights move and swirl, radiant yet translucent in nature.

- Picture the colors merging into a rich, sparkling blue-black hue. Hold this image in your mind. Consider that this sapphire energy has the power to ease and transform negative emotions in you.

- As you breathe in, imagine this deep blue light filling you, capturing and transforming all the anger and hatred in your heart, mind, and body. This deep blue light makes it possible to understand, accept, and let go of the knot of anger and hatred, transmuting its sour venom.

- Feel the breath come in and go out, in and out. Keep full awareness on the in-breath, full awareness on the out-breath. If you have any pain or sickness, let the deep blue sparkling light go to that area, and experience it benefiting you.

- Now bring your attention to the out-breath, imagining anger and hatred leaving the body with each breath. All of it is transformed into a dirty, unhealthy-looking black smoke. Watch this dissolve out in front of you, away from your body. Feel how the dark-colored smoke is being expelled with the out-breath.

- Continue breathing in this way (at least ten minutes) until you feel the knot of anger loosening, the toxic emotions leaving your body, mind, and heart. You can do this by saying to yourself, *Breathing in, I receive deep blue sparkling light. Breathing out, I let go of all unnecessary anger and old resentments.* With each breath, notice the negative emotions washing away, dissipating and evaporating into the air. Then say: *In, calming deep blue* with the in-breath and *Out, releasing old smoke* with the out-breath.

- At the end of the sitting, when your resentments and anger have ebbed, let the sapphire light go out first to people you know and then to all others.

- Then picture the blue-black light returning to the sphere, merging again with all the other colors. Watch it move away from you until it completely vanishes in space. Afterward, breathe in tranquility and let your mind linger for as long as you wish.

- In order to untie a knot of strong anger, try this practice each day for one week. If any tension arises, do the Deep Breathing, Sitting Meditation, or Hello Old Friend exercises given in earlier chapters before returning to this practice.

You may want to take a few moments to jot down key insights or images that emerged during this meditation here or in your Personal Log.

_____

_____

_____

_____

VARIATION: COLORS FOR OTHER FEELINGS

You can use this same practice to loosen other mental knots—such as jealousy, discontent, delusions, or cravings—by using a different color for each one. Let your investigation into self-awareness surface which knot needs to be worked on in yourself and, consequently, which color you will use in the meditation. The following colors are suggested in the ancient Vedic and Tantric traditions:

- *Green light to ease jealousy.*
  In Vedic tradition, green is believed to neutralize resentment and encourage positive self-expression.

- *Yellow light to ease restless discontent.*
  Yellow is said to aid in curing worry or frustration and to support self-assertion.

- *Sky-blue light to ease delusion.*
  This color is associated with insight into problems and promotes contemplation and communication.

- *Ruby-red light to counteract craving.*
  Deep red is said to reduce fear and temper the depression and sadness of yearning. Vedic tradition holds that the color red helps sustain initiative and courage.

THINGS TO WATCH FOR

- *You worry that thinking about negative emotions will make you feel worse.*
  In this practice, we *do* turn our attention to negative feelings such as anger, jealousy, or craving—in order to work with them and relax their grip on our psyche. At first, it may seem to intensify these feelings. That's okay. They will pass. You are becoming more aware. Noticing knots of negative emotion is not harmful unless you dwell on them. Replaying painful incidents time and again in your mind—a kind of obsessive thinking—can by itself trigger an amygdala hijack. If you find yourself doing this, refer back to chapter 5, Accepting What You Feel, or apply a visualization of colored light to ease the knot of pain or discontent.

- *You notice that the knot of negativity doesn't seem to loosen.*
  If, during this meditation, the knot of anger or pain does not diminish, it suggests that the feeling or internal formation is perhaps deep and long-standing. It may be that you need to come to a fuller acceptance of the negative feeling—perhaps you are judging yourself in subtle ways you have not yet

noticed. In this case, return to the practices in chapter 5 and work with them for several weeks before returning to this practice.

Or it may be that you have not yet uncovered the root cause of the knot. Perhaps an early-life experience or underlying mental stance is feeding your negative emotion, and so it stays with you in stubborn defiance of your efforts to release it. In this case, return to the practices in chapter 6, Looking Deeply, and work with them before returning to this practice.

- *You experience undue tension while working with this practice.*

  Experiencing some discomfort, at first, while applying this practice is normal—few of us enjoy touching a knot of "ugly" emotion. If, however, you experience intense anxiety or panic when approaching this practice, you should stop immediately. In this case, consider working with a psychologist to get more support for letting go of old patterns in your emotional life.

DEVELOPING PROACTIVE POISE

If we want to stay poised in the long term, we need to develop the part of the brain that can override the amygdala's signals—the left prefrontal lobe. The irrefutable means toward this end is meditation. In earlier chapters, we learned mindful breathing and sitting meditation, and here we add Mountain Meditation to our repertoire.

Humanity has long looked to nature for inspiration, solace, and renewal, and mountains—sacred in cultures around the world—speak to us with their majestic, quiet strength. In this meditation, a mountain image is held in the mind's eye as we sit, still, emulating its resolute immobility. First, we picture the mountain, absorbing its attributes with a "beginner's mind," full of awe and wonder and curiosity. We see how the mountain—pelted by rain, blanketed in snow, struck by lightning, or scorched by the sun—remains undaunted. Laden with ice. Whipped by wind. Through it all, the mountain sits. When spring returns, leaves sprout and creatures feast from the mountain's bounty—and still she sits, immobile, steadfast. In this meditation, we, too, are nourished by the energy of the mountain.

In addition to the calm we gain from observing and intuiting the mountain's presence in nature, there is a still deeper intimation, here exemplified by an ancient Zen koan (a poem or statement that cannot be completely understood by the rational mind):

> After sitting, a monk asked Great Master Yueh-shan Hung-tao, "What are you thinking [sitting there] so fixedly?" The master answered, "I'm thinking of not-thinking." The monk asked, "How can one think of not-thinking?" The master said, "Non-thinking."[20]

Dosho Port-sensei sheds light on the nuances found in the original Chinese ideograms. The word *fixedly*, meaning "still still sitting," he says, consists of two characters: *kotsu kotsu*, the first *kanji* (calligraphic character), depicts a mountain with a flat top—open and vulnerable—representing a state of acceptance. The

second character, *chi*, describes an earthy foundation—
an ever-present, steadfast grounding. Together, these
characters suggest a deeper meaning about the age-old
koan: that "still still sitting" is to be like a mountain,
solid and rooted in the earth yet exposed to the elements. True strength is both. This is the subtle lesson of
the Mountain Meditation.

PRACTICE

IMAGING A STILL MOUNTAIN[21]

This meditation can be practiced as described, or
adapted to your own vision of the mountain and its
meaning. Although it can be done in any posture, the
recommended method involves sitting on a cushion on
the floor, cross-legged, mountainlike. Actually looking
at a mountain may be helpful, but is not necessary.

WHAT YOU'LL NEED

- Ten to twenty minutes to complete the practice.

- A quiet place to sit. Take a comfortable position where
  you can breathe easily and keep an alert mind, sitting
  so that your body is relaxed and your spine is straight.

- Your Personal log.

TRY THIS

- Begin this meditation with five minutes of mindful
  breathing. Relax and breathe deeply from your
  diaphragm. Each out-breath is a feeling of deeper
  relaxation and release of tension.

- Picture the most magnificent mountain you have seen or can imagine. Notice its peak, its angles, the rocky base growing up out of the earth. Perhaps you see it in the crisp light of day, snow glaze dripped down its peaks, trees thickening to evergreen darkness down the slopes to its granite foot.

- Notice its massive strength, its unmoving nature, and its pervasive calm. Breathe with the image, taking in its strength, meeting its power and tranquility. Solid, still, complete.

- When you feel ready, bring a sense of the mountain into your own body. You and the mountain of the mind's eye become one. Your head becomes the lofty peak; your shoulders and arms the sides of the mountain; your buttocks and legs the solid base rooted to your cushion on the floor or to your chair. Experience the upright, lifted quality of the mountain moving from the base deep in your spine up to the top of your head.

- Morning gives way to late day and you are warmed by the sun. Green turns yellow and red and white, deep blue at night. And so it goes. The moon rises and yet you are still. You sit. Yourself.

- Breathe deeply, unmoving, unprovoked by the onslaughts of storm or sleet or rainfall. Notice the seasons change from bleak ice to verdant spring. See how the mountain sits. Detached, weathering. The conditions of nature pass, one into the other, touching only the surface of the mount. Its strength is much deeper. Solid. Calm.

- Go to the top of your mountain mind, the place that breaks through beyond the clouds where the sun is visible once again—opening your view. From this crest, look at your life down in the valley, out on the plains, noting any shifts in perspective you may experience.

- Now complete the meditation with five minutes of breathing in resolute, empowering calm. You can do this by saying to yourself, *Breathing in, mountain. Breathing out, solid.* Then: *In, mountain* with the in-breath and *Out, solid* with the out-breath.

You may want to take a few moments to jot down your emerging thoughts and images in your Personal Log. Consider these questions for reflection:

What weather conditions prevailed in my image of the mountain? Storm, lightning, hail, pelted by freezing rain, or sweet breezes and misting rain?

_____

_____

_____

_____

What does this "weather" represent in my life? For example, what "weather" is assailing me right now?

_____

_____

_____

_____

How does the mountain image suggest new ways of carrying myself in times of turmoil?

_____

_____

_____

As Jon Kabat-Zinn, in *Wherever You Go, There You Are,* says:

> By becoming the mountain in our meditation, we can link up with its strength and stability, and adopt them for our own. We can use its energies to support our efforts to encounter each moment with mindfulness, equanimity, and clarity.[22]

In stillness, the mountain presents a model for "weathering" the thunder and lightning of conflict, and the rain that falls on our emotional lives. With time and practice, you can absorb its timeless strength.

Each of the practices in this chapter, Staying Poised, enables us to steady ourselves against the sudden gust of an amygdala hijack. By developing the capacity to remain calm, we are less likely to overreact and become triggered in a stressful moment as well as in the hours, even days that follow.

The habit of drawing a Circle of Protection around ourselves calls forth deeper wisdom, compassion, and appropriate action in the face of threats or fear. In Releasing Mental Knots, we draw on ancient medicinal techniques and visualize colored light to penetrate our habitual mental knots, easing their destructive power and tempering our negativity. In Mountain Meditation, we soak up the rooted, solid energy of a mountain, becoming more deeply aware that our reactions come and go like stormy, blustering gales. By practicing daily meditation, we take steps on our own behalf, building new pathways to greater peace of mind.

Once you are versed in these practices, you can expand your repertoire even further by creating your own images—personal cues—to signal a change in direction, alerting your brain to send impulses down an alternative route.

T R A I L M A R K E R

At this rest stop, you can look back and see how your automatic habits of reaction—deeply ingrained neural pathways worn smooth and deep from years of frequent use—lead you down the same old road to the same undesirable end. And how crucial it is to interrupt this firing flow of neural impulses.

In order to set a different course, you have learned ways to further stillness in your mind; to counteract the paralyzing grip of fear; and to penetrate old knots of hatred, jealousy, or delusion. Each of these practices builds poise by re-engaging the thinking brain, enabling you to *pause* before instigating needless squabbles, *hesitate* before lashing out, and *stop* before doing harm to others. Although it is only natural and human to experience negative emotions, greater poise—grace under pressure—prevents you from being ruled by them and frees you to take a step in a new direction.

Now you are ready to embrace the challenge and ulti-mate goal of your efforts: better relationships with others. Less clouded by the haze of your internal formations and mental knots, you can see others more clearly. You are able to meet *them*. Love *them*. Work with *them*.

Although separated here for clarity's sake, the boundary between Self and Other is often hard to discern. Farther on down the way, you may begin to see that all along you have been clearing the road toward deeper understanding and harmony with others. Working on Self and working with Others is one continuous, intertwining path up the mountain.

PART THREE

OTHER

CHAPTER 8

DEEPENING EMPATHY

> Know the world of nature of which you are a part, and
> you will be yourself and know yourself without thought
> or effort. The things you see you are.
>
> ARISTOTLE

The heart of better relationships is empathy—the willingness to tune in to the feelings of others, sense their
unspoken concerns, and understand their needs. Long
promoted by all major religions of the world, compassion is too often obscured by calls to righteous anger
and vengeful justice. Yet few capabilities are as powerful
as this tenderness of heart.

When we think about the people we are close to, the
importance of empathy is easy to see. We live together
in similar emotional territory, sharing interests, desires,
and beliefs. In our intimate personal relationships,
even when we disagree, we often make the effort to see
our beloved's point of view. But due to the dark side of
human nature, empathy is not a "given" in all relationships. Greed, anger, and ignorance seem to rise endlessly in this world of human affairs. The briefest
perusal of the morning paper or half an hour of nightly
news testifies to this. In the world of acquaintances and
strangers—and even among family and friends—

empathy can fade into another cherished ideal, an unrealistic utopian fantasy.

But the news is not all bad. We are also from time to time reminded of our exquisite humanity. Often, profound tragedy brings out the best of the human heart.

After the attacks on the World Trade Center and the Pentagon, we confronted an example of the violent disregard for life that has become all too common in the modern world. Yet it was immediately followed by an unprecedented display of charitable giving, heroic acts by rescue workers, and a worldwide outpouring of grief—examples too numerous to mention. A friend was in Paris when the attacks happened:

> *On September 14, the whole of Europe came to a standstill for three minutes. On this international day of mourning, all radio stations on the continent played John Lennon's "Imagine" at twelve noon. I was on my way to lunch when everyone who was driving pulled over. People came out of the shops and restaurants, and we all just stood in the street, silent and still, listening to the song. It was moving—an entire modern metropolis frozen, reflecting on what it means to be human, alive, together.*

Certain events, both large and small, offer glimpses into the depth and breadth of our connection to one another. We see the "better angels of our nature"[1]—the qualities of the human soul, the legacy built into our genes—that thrive on cooperation and interdependence. Recognizing this heritage, we can expand our ability to empathize beyond the familiar territory of our intimates. David Loy, in *Indra's Postmodern Net*, expresses this sentiment in an echo of the biblical golden rule: "I shall indeed love my neighbor as myself when I experience that I *am* my neighbor." Empathy is tuning in to the world beyond ourselves, penetrating the veil of separation between "us" and "them."

In reality, we are mentally, emotionally, and physically living in a world of interbeing with *all* others, not only those we know and love. The things we see, we are. For thousands of years, spiritual teachers in the East have used the image of a vast net of energy to describe how we are linked to one another.

The original ancient text refers to this web as the Jewel Net of Indra, named for the Indian deity of creation. It goes like this:

This [Net of Indra] is made of jewels: because the jewels are clear, they reflect each other's images, appearing in each other's reflections upon reflection, ad infinitum, all appearing at once in each jewel. . . .

This jewel can show the reflections of all the jewels all at once—and just as this is so of this jewel, so it is of every other jewel: the reflection is multiplied and remultiplied over and over endlessly.

These infinitely multiplying jewel reflections are all in one jewel and show clearly—the others do not hinder this. If you sit in one jewel, then you are sitting in all the jewels in every direction. Why? Because in one jewel there are all the jewels.[2]

In this myth, the jewel represents each one of us, made of the same material, reflecting each other, intimately connected in every moment. A web of interbeing. When any one of us in the net is touched—even the smallest vibration at any one point—all others "in the ten directions" feel the tremor.

Although it may be tempting to dismiss this old story

as a beautiful, poetic metaphor, the Jewel Net embodies ancient, intuitive knowledge. Thousands of years after this story was written, we recognize the uncanny resemblance to our modern world of instant satellite communication and fiber-optic cable. There is a hidden universe that reflects this image as well—a world of particles and microorganisms. In a sense, empathy is the electrochemical bond, the invisible connective tissue that holds the stuff of life together.

We take for granted the existence of solid objects. But if we could, by some subtle rearrangement of our senses, see the world of elements, it would be little more than a constant movement of infinitely tiny particles forming atoms, molecules, and cells. These miraculous arrangements allow us to perceive walls, windows, books, and words. Our current understanding of subatomic particles reveals a universe not made of separate, individual particles, but rather one in which individual particles act as a single entity:

> In quantum physics, which concerns itself with the smallest dimensions of the physical world, several experiments . . . have revealed the existence of what are termed *nonlocal* events. Briefly: If two subatomic particles that have been in contact are separated, a change in one is correlated with a change in the other, instantly and to the same degree, no matter how far apart they may be.[3]

Particles change simultaneously and mysteriously. We don't yet know how they communicate with each other, but they do. No matter how great the distance, they can change *together*, instantaneously. They seem to understand each other. Call it quantum empathy.

A similar "acting together" takes place in the world of microorganisms. Bacteria, the oldest and simplest life-forms, sense their environment—heat, light, acidity, magnetic fields—and talk to each other in the language of DNA. By exchanging information, individual organisms—be they cells, ants, or people—form communities that become new, composite life-forms. The ability to pool resources seems to be a universal quality in nature, the origin of complexity in all living things—molecules and fish schools, anthills and urban centers.[4]

The wonders of the hidden universe offer insight into the characteristics of *human* nature. We are an extension of all this subatomic and microscopic "empathizing," and we, in turn, are part of a larger shared consciousness, a oneness that creates the whole. Yet these connections are often eclipsed by the convolutions of human interaction. Lewis Thomas, in *Lives of a Cell*, puts it this way: "Although we are by all odds the most social of all the social animals—more interdependent, more attached to each other, more inseparable in our behavior than bees—we do not often feel our conjoined intelligence."[5] Whether we are particles, microbes, ants, or people, one thing seems clear: We cannot *not* affect each other. Recognizing that reality is the ultimate goal of empathy. We are all in this together.

Though it is inspiring to see patterns of cooperation in nature, our very human world is thick with the smoke and noise of suffering. Too often, we feel there is little we can do. And yet deepening our capacity for empathy requires a heart that holds the concerns of others. "When we want to understand something, we cannot just stand outside and observe it. We have to enter deeply into it and be one with it in order to really understand. If we want to understand a person, we have to feel his feelings, suffer his sufferings, and enjoy his joy."[6] Only when we can recognize our own face in the mirror of others will we have compassion for what moves and hinders them.

Feeling with the experience of others depends on a profound understanding of the subtlety and range of our *own* fears, desires, and needs. To do this, we need to use our emotional intelligence-gathering network, bringing clarity to the static of human interaction. If we can't hear our own feelings, we are likely to be "off key" when responding to others, emotionally "tone deaf" to the sound of their needs.[7]

Sometimes misreading a situation causes a little dissonance:

> *A couple, newly engaged and still madly in love, rented a cabin for a weekend getaway to hike amid the autumn colors along the North Shore of Lake Superior. The cabin's picture window faced the lake. Two large oak trees stood near the water framing the view, with branches leaning out over the water—a perfect scene. Inside, they sipped wine to the backdrop music of the fire, softly touched their lips, and basked in nature's silent beauty. After a long pause, she asked him what he was thinking about . . .*
>
> *"Well," he said, pointing, "see that branch out there?"*
> *"Mmm-hmm." Her eyes narrowed a little.*
> *"I was just wondering how far I could get out on that thing, you know, before I'd fall."*

At other times, misreading a situation carries serious consequences—far worse than a dashed moment of romance. When we are too distracted, too busy, or too absorbed in our own self-interest—immersed in old habits of "tuning out"—the effects can be anything from the crossed wires of miscommunication to damaged relationships to the breakdown of diplomatic talks. In these situations, empathy repairs our connections and restores our relationships.

The key to developing empathy lies in honing our brain's interpersonal radar.

THE NEUROLOGY OF EMPATHY

Human beings have a remarkable capacity for nuances in communication, both spoken and unspoken. Our brain's design—for reasons vital to our survival—

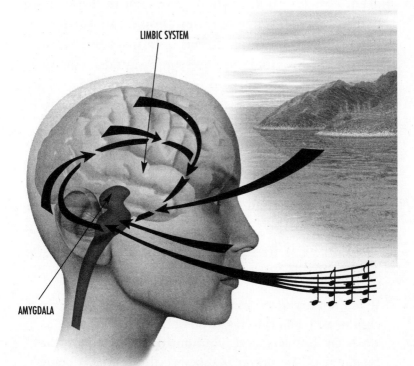

LIMBIC SYSTEM

AMYGDALA

Figure 8.1
The emotional brain is an open-loop system

enables us to pick up on and be affected by the joys and sorrows of others in our world. We are "wired" for connection. The reason one person's mood can affect the emotions of people nearby is due to the "open-loop" nature of the emotional brain. This open loop is part of our genetic heritage, rooted in the necessity for a mother to be constantly aware, intuitively, of her child's needs. But this ability is not limited to the mother–child bond.

This same open-loop design of the limbic system enables us to be affected by the thoughts and intentions of others, even from afar. A moment of silence in a large group of people—in a stadium, for example, or at a funeral—offers a glimpse into the phenomenon of shared, concentrated thought. Even more astonishing is that just the presence of other people can impact our physiology. Recent research has demonstrated the startling conclusion that one person's signals "can alter hormone levels, cardiovascular functions, sleep rhythms, even immune functions, inside the body of another."[8]

Consider, too, the act of prayer for someone who is ill. Remarkable research shows that holding kind and loving thoughts for another can help the person recover. In more than 130 scientific studies in the general area of healing, the positive effect of prayer was strongly indicated, regardless of the religious tradition of those praying.

> When put to the test in actual experiments in hospitals, clinics and laboratories, distant prayer *does have an effect*—in humans and nonhumans, even when the recipient of the prayer is unaware the prayer is being offered.[9]

The notion that our emotional communication—even the slightest vibration of it in the Jewel Net—produces measurable change in others is cause for deep pause and reflection.

What we are truly striving for, however, is more than the occasional "good thought" for another. True empathy is the ability to "feel with" others who are different from ourselves.

OUR CAPACITY FOR EMPATHY

Empathic people have the ability to attune to others on a physiological *and* emotional level, involving a finely tuned physical synchrony with another. Here it may help to recall your work in chapter 3, Tuning In, as the ability to tune in to your own internal state is now extended to another. Just as we learned to tune in to what our own bodies are telling us—physically and emotionally—we now develop this ability to "read" others.

Being in tune with our own bodies forms the basis for feeling the moods of others. We don't normally carry around a blinking, beeping heart monitor for use in daily conversation, but we can develop the necessary equipment to keep an eye on the emotional vital signs of others. Deepening our empathy involves sharpening our mind–body connection. If we want to work on deepening our empathy for someone else, we must first start at a physical level—attuning our body to the other person, sensing the tension, anger, sorrow, or loneliness in his or her breathing, posture, and movement. Then we listen intuitively to what those sensations say to our own mind and heart about the person's emotional experience.

When we do this, several key challenges arise:

- If we are having a heated reaction ourselves—when the emotional brain is driving the body with a strong reaction of fear or anger—there can be little or no empathy. Here we need to call upon the self-management skills discussed in chapter 7, Staying Poised. If we are not tuned in, we are unable to put aside our own agenda and quiet the noise in our mind. More than just being distracted, we risk projecting our "emotional baggage" onto others and misreading them entirely.

- When we don't see eye to eye with people, we may be concerned that empathizing implies we condone their action. Rather, empathy means we can see the issues or concerns that lie behind another's feelings, but we need *not* agree with them. Understanding someone's point of view does not require us to embrace it.

- Empathy for people we love is the most evident form of this skill. Although not always true, feeling with a loved one is usually easier than having empathy for casual acquaintances or strangers. More difficult is being open to the cares and perspective of those we see as enemies. This requires great determination and a belief that empathy is both a spiritual good and a practical means to better relationships.

Despite these challenges, we can build our capacity for kindness for others. In the words of the Dalai Lama,

"We all have compassion: we want to free others from suffering. And, to some degree, we all love and want others to be happy. These feelings may not be very strong or extensive, but everyone has them in some measure."[10] Some of us experience this only in fleeting moments—twinges of identification with our shared human condition. When we pay attention to these spontaneous moments of compassion, the pathways for empathic behavior become stronger.

Building this skill opens us to the idea that we are interconnected at an emotional and neurological level. Just as the brilliant design of our hands allows us to grasp and maneuver objects in the physical world, empathy acts as the "opposable thumb" of the psyche, helping us to take hold of each other when the going gets tough.

EMPATHY AT WORK

In times of conflict, the ability to reach out to others can be powerful magic. It happened for a company I worked with in London. The firm was owned by a conglomerate headquartered in Germany and employed people from fourteen different nations. They hired my colleagues and me to mediate an impasse among the professional staff, support staff, and management. In the past year, a group from headquarters had replaced the former British management team in a flurry of cost-cutting measures. Sales, morale, and production were at an all-time low. The company had lost 40 percent of its talent in one year. Resentment and distrust were rampant, exacerbated by a historical, cultural distrust of the new German management team.

The turning point of our intervention was a three-day staff retreat in the English countryside. After a difficult first day, we spontaneously created a role-reversal activity the next morning. Each group (upper management, midmanagement, consultants, and support staff) was assigned to take the viewpoint of a different group and "walk in their shoes." We posed questions about how they thought others viewed them in the firm, what obstacles they faced, and what they needed to do their best work in the company. After completing the questions, they shared answers from their newly acquired perspectives.

In the second part of the exercise, the groups all returned to their real-life roles and were asked to rate the accuracy of the answers, then elaborate on any additional feelings and concerns that had not been covered during the role play. In the end, most of the employees and management were shocked at how well others really *did* understand them, despite positional and cultural differences. The activity was a success, but the most poignant moment came when the almost universally hated company controller, called the "ax-man" behind his back, welled up with tears and said he couldn't believe that others understood his situation as well as they did.

Once people had connected on a human level—practicing empathy for each other—we could go on to discuss the policy and management practices that were necessary to restore a positive work environment. There were still substantive problems and disagreements, but we were able to maintain a constructive momentum for seeking better solutions. One year later, no one had left the firm, and results matched business plan projections.

The opportunities for opening a deeper understanding abound in each present moment. Perhaps it will give us hope to recall the Dalai Lama's words that "anyone who has good thoughts, who does a lot to help others, and leaves behind good memories is respected by people all over the world, whether [he or she] is religious or not."[11]

DEEPENING YOUR COMPASSION

"I think that empathy is important ... when dealing with others on any level. If you're having some difficulties, it's extremely helpful to be able to try to put yourself in the other person's place and see how you would react to the situation. Even if you have no common experience with the other person or have a very different lifestyle, you can try to do this through imagination.... This helps you develop an awareness and respect for another's feelings, which is an important factor in reducing conflicts and problems with other people."[12] This wisdom from the Dalai Lama speaks to the value of the following practice: Exchanging Yourself with Another. It opens the heart to places beyond the "small world" of our own activities, deepens our capacity for empathy, and benefits our relationships with others.

The practice comes from the ancient tradition of Lo-jong or "thought training," originated by Gautama Buddha and passed to us over the past twenty-five hundred years. In that era, people had not heard of neuropathways in the brain but they knew from experience that the mind affects how we feel and act. Hence, they counsel us to train our thoughts—etch new pathways—to cultivate deeper empathy with others. This, in turn, leads to greater harmony in our lives and in our world.

Exchanging Yourself with Another is a core practice of thought training. In the original text, the power of this practice is said to be "like a diamond, in that even its fragments excel every other jewel."[13] Working with this practice imbues our jewel in the Net of Indra with human warmth and a deeper understanding of others. Cleared of stubborn resentments, unsullied by rigid intolerance, free from delusions of difference, we can indeed radiate kindheartedness. Over time, this practice helps us see others more clearly, closer to who they "really are," and opens a path for deeper empathy and understanding in our relationships at work and at home.

Known as a "reversal exercise" in Western psychology, this practice builds on the nonjudgmental orientation suggested in chapter 5, Accepting What You Feel. It instructs us to choose people whom we wish to understand more deeply and "exchange" ourselves with them—breathing as they breathe, feeling what they feel, taking on their mind-set and view of the world. "This technique involves the capacity to temporarily suspend . . . your own viewpoint [and] look from the other person's perspective, to imagine what would be the situation if you were in his shoes."[14]

PRACTICE

 EXCHANGING YOURSELF WITH ANOTHER

This exercise involves meditative writing, where you reverse roles and "become" another person. Choose someone you would like to understand more deeply as the focus of this activity.

WHAT YOU'LL NEED

- Fifteen to twenty minutes to complete the practice.

- A quiet place to sit. For sitting meditation, sit in a chair or on the floor so that your body is relaxed and your spine is straight.

- Your Personal Log.

TRY THIS

- Take the first five minutes to breathe mindfully. Feel your breath come in and go out, in and out. Keep full awareness on the in-breath, full awareness on the out-breath . . . then start the practice.

- Take the next few moments to focus on *receiving* acceptance and compassion into yourself. Begin by visualizing a figure of compassion, someone you know or a figure from your own cultural or spiritual tradition, just as you did in the Circle of Protection practice.

- Picture this compassion figure standing or seated on a chair adorned with precious jewels, smiling beautifully and radiating golden light. The palm of her right hand rests on her right knee. Her left hand holds a bowl filled with nectar resting in her lap. The nectar represents the insights that clear our clouded states of mind.

- This figure's warm gaze looks at us with total acceptance. Her whole being radiates love and omniscience streaming from her heart to ours. These rays fill us with courage and strength to successfully complete the practice of Exchanging Ourselves with Another.

- Now think of a person you would like to understand more deeply. Recall his face, smell, and voice. Close your eyes and imagine him standing in a familiar setting, facing you. Picture yourself bowing to him, or nodding your head in acknowledgment, mentally asking his permission to "visit" in order to understand him better.

- Begin to imagine seeing the world through the other person's point of view. With your mind's eye, go inside that person's body and let yourself explore—notice the feelings, thoughts, and sensations you experience as you "try on" his mind-set. Stay with this for a few moments, seeing through his eyes, walking in his shoes.

- Open your eyes and take the next ten minutes to reflect on the following questions *as if* you were the other person:

  ~ *How am I feeling physically?*

  _____

  _____

  _____

  ~ *What is my mood state?*

  _____

  _____

  _____

  ~ *What are my most pressing emotional needs right now?*

  _____

  _____

  _____

~ Is there anything causing me sadness or agitation? How am I thinking about the situation that has brought about this distress?

_____

_____

_____

~ What is important for me to say to the person I am "visiting"?

_____

_____

_____

- Now close your eyes once again, coming back to your breathing. Focus on breathing in and breathing out, deeply and mindfully. Return to a clear sense of yourself, the solidness of your own body, the feeling of the cushion or chair under your seat, the firm ground supporting your feet.

- Pause and hold the other person (the person you thought about in this meditation) in your mind's eye, making a strong wish for the causes of his suffering to be removed, for any and all emotional distress to be consoled.

- Next, send him the energy of happiness and kind understanding. Emanating from our heart, it touches him and transforms him according to his personal need. With the out-breath, exhale loving-kindness, saturating the entire space around you, spreading, touching every living being. Do this for several moments.

- Finally, allow a moment of silence and stillness before getting up. Slowly move your hands and feet; feel the wholeness of your body again before returning to your day's routine. You may want to pause and capture key insights from this meditation in your Personal Log.

In conclusion, reflect on how you and the other person, along with all others—friends, loved ones, and enemies—are part of the Jewel Net, not separate and different after all.

TUNING IN TO ANOTHER

When her daughter was a two-and-a-half-pound newborn, the asthma started. The medications the doctors prescribed seemed to have little effect. Her sweet one lay there, gasping and choking for air. Distraught and aching to help her daughter, she tried something novel—nothing she had ever read about in the baby books. Later she would reflect, "I don't know how I thought of doing it; I just followed my instincts, my intuition as a mother."

Picking up her tiny babe, she held her close to her heart, rocking and breathing peace into her child. "I would start by breathing shallow, like she was, and then go deeper with each breath," she said. "It was almost like the calmness would go out through my skin and into her, like an infusion from me to her. Breathing love into her, I was able to bring her back to normal."

They continued this, mother and child, until her

daughter was four years old. "When an asthma attack would start, I would say, 'Time to breathe,' and hold her—not as close as when she was a baby, but near," the mother told me. "She was sucking and struggling so hard to breathe that the soft spot in between her collarbone would collapse and her face would be contorted and pale. I could feel the panic in her. As we would start to breathe in, breathe out, getting deeper and calmer with each breath, I held her in my heart."

Depending on the severity of the asthma attack, they would breathe together for anywhere from ten to twenty minutes. Her daughter's face and limbs would relax, her cheeks a healthy pink once again. "She would hop off my lap and go back to playing with her dolls or whatever she was doing."

By the age of four, her daughter could "breathe herself down" from an asthma attack. Now she is seventeen, an accomplished young athlete. "The doctors say she is one of the most self-managed asthmatics they have ever seen," her mother says. "She uses her inhaler once in a while, but very rarely.

"Equally as precious to me is the fact that my daughter and I have remained close through her growing-up years. We have a profound connection, a bond-beyond-words."

In chapter 3, Tuning In, we used deep breathing to raise awareness of our emotions and where our body holds tension—a technique to help us connect more deeply with ourselves. Here we expand that practice, breathing in rhythm with others to deepen our connection *with them*.

This stunningly simple practice can be quite moving. Its origins lie in Eastern Tantric practice, a branch of Vedic spiritual studies in India. Unfortunately, in both the West and the East, Tantric practices are mistakenly identified with sex, the pursuit of ecstasy, and pretzel-like yogic postures—sometimes giving Tantra a bad name. In reality, the word *Tantra* comes from the root *tan*, "to weave, to expand, or to spread." Practices from the Tantric tradition were intended to deepen and reweave meaningful connections with others and with nature, restoring the Jewel Net of creation.

The practice of Breathing with One You Love increases our emotional sensitivity, physical tenderness, or sexual intimacy with one we hold dear. It is not intended to be foreplay, but rather a form of connection in and of itself. Tuning in, breathing together, and being in sync opens channels of understanding at a profound, nonverbal level. There are times when deep emotional closeness can be more satisfying, more touching than the act of intercourse.

We can breathe in rhythm with another by simply standing or sitting nearby and tuning in, matching the person's in-breath and out-breath at a physical level. More often, this practice is done while holding hands, caressing, embracing, or comforting your loved one. Entwining breaths, hearts beating as one, minds touching.

PRACTICES

BREATHING WITH ONE YOU LOVE

Just breathing *with* another develops closeness in your relationship. It increases your sensitivity to the other person, nurtures tender feelings, and builds pathways of greater empathy. Although simple, it is a deeply spiritual experience: sharing breath, giving and receiving love. As such, this practice is intended for use within a committed and loving relationship, with either a partner, a child, or an infirm family member.

WHAT YOU'LL NEED

- Fifteen to twenty minutes to complete the practice.

- Quiet, uninterrupted time with your loved one.

TRY THIS

- Sitting or lying across from the other person, begin by individually tuning in to your own breathing. Notice it come in and go out, in and out. Let the breath just happen, observing it wherever and how- ever you feel it—a rise and fall of your belly, a cool- ness in your nose, a pressure in your lungs... breathing, with no goal or agenda in mind.

- Breathe in deeply, filling your lungs. Exhale slowly, letting go of lingering tension from your day. Take a deep breath, then slowly exhale. Do this for several minutes, centering yourself, clearing yourself of dis- tractions and noise.

- Now turn attention to your loved one—standing or sitting near her, sharing touch, if you wish. You can embrace, lightly stroke her back or arm, or sit cross- legged apart from each other—touching hands, holding eye contact, sharing a cloak of silence.

- Begin to breathe with your loved one, as she does. As she breathes in, you breathe in. As she breathes out, you breathe out. Match her in-breath and out-breath at a physical level. Tune in to her—recognize her in-

breath and breathe in. Recognize her out-breath and
breathe out.

• Once you are in rhythm with your beloved, try
breathing alternately—when she breathes in, you
breathe out. When she breathes out, you breathe in.
This will teach you to attune to the other person's
breathing and more subtle levels of connection.
Experience the oneness, channeling your internal
energy into connecting with the other person.

• Return to breathing in sync with the other person.
As she breathes in, you breathe in. As she breathes
out, you breathe out. Match her in-breath and out-
breath at a physical level. Take your time. Relax and
enjoy. Notice the closeness of your bodies and minds,
the powerful union of energy that occurs with this
simple act of breathing with the one you love.

• Try doing this for five or ten minutes every morning
or evening with someone you love, someone you
wish to be closer to emotionally, for several weeks.
This will deepen your capacity for empathy and prepare you to "breathe with" another in a more difficult situation such as illness or injury.

DOING TONG-LEN: AN ADVANCED BREATHING PRACTICE

If you are comfortable and proficient at Breathing with
One You Love, you can try a more advanced breathing
practice to develop compassion. Called Tong-len, it
means "the practice of giving and taking"—a corner-
stone of Tibetan meditative practices for opening the
heart. It begins with a true desire to understand and

help others by first developing empathy for ourselves
and then extending that out to others. If we are in a
stance of compassion, our own knots of anger, frustration, fear, or craving become links to understanding
others more deeply.

Although I will introduce it here, I don't advise doing
deep Tong-len work without the guidance of a spiritual
teacher, minister, or psychologist versed in this method.
Particularly in the beginning, there is the risk of
absorbing too much of the other person's distress. A
guide will help prevent this and ensure the technique is
practiced properly.

The practice of Giving and Taking refers to the visualization practice of giving your own happiness to other
beings and taking upon yourself all their suffering:

- With the exhalation of the breath, send the other
  person happiness in the form of rays of light, surrounding him and infusing him with consolation.

- With the in-breath, take his emotional distress or suffering into yourself. Imagine a cloud of darkness that
  is consumed by the radiance and kindness of your
  heart.

- Breathe out any residue of distress that remains,
  seeing it expelled in the form of dark, ashy smoke
  that is transmuted into the light of happiness. Pause
  and extend this light of happiness back to the other
  person. Then picture it spreading and flooding all
  other living beings.

- When you are finished meditating on Giving and
  Taking, spend the last few minutes breathing mindfully and returning to yourself. Let go of the pains

and sorrows of the other person, shifting your attention back to the activities of your day.

TRAIL MARKER

In the first half of this book, you worked to override the brain's built-in system to alert you to danger or threat. Now you have tapped into another feature of our brain's design—its penchant for cooperation and connection. You are more equipped to walk in that world of others, to understand them and respond constructively, empathically, compassionately.

Empathy is a powerful force, a wireless web that connects us all. You have become more aware of this web's existence and power—the power of an infinite number of jewels reflecting all other jewels. At this overlook, stop to take in the panorama. Enjoy the view. Imagine this: Everything you see, you are—one net of interbeing.

Think for a few moments about putting empathy into practice in your life:

Whom do I wish to understand more fully? Choose one or two people to focus on at first.

_____

_____

_____

_____

What insights do I have from "putting myself in their shoes"?

_____

_____

_____

Everything you have done so far forms a necessary progression of steps *so that* you can be more effective in day-to-day interactions, friendships, and relationships with loved ones. The next chapter talks of aligning your actions with your deepened compassion, looking at what you do and say when having conflict with another.

In order to make the best use of the practices to come, consider:

Which of my important relationships are conflicted at this time?

_____

_____

_____

_____

How would I like them to be different? What is my picture of greater harmony in these relationships?

_____

_____

_____

_____

Hold this desire in mind as you walk through the next chapter.

CHAPTER 9

LIVING IN HARMONY

Our life is not about sitting on some mountaintop contemplating our navel. It takes place in the world, interacting with others.

JOHN DAIDO LOORI[1]

So far, we have been securing the solid footing of *our*
awareness and *our* poise, balancing ourselves with the
open arms of *our* compassion. But the benefits resonate
far beyond *us*. They're about interacting with others.
With a firm base established, we can now build the skills
and construct the relationship habits that promote harmony with others. Indeed, we can sparkle in the vast,
prescient Jewel Net of Indra.

Without this foundation of inner work, seminars on
conflict resolution, parenting, team building, or any
other aspects of human relations will not help us hold
the ground we have gained. Communication techniques are of little use if not supported by empathy and
self-control. We will be unable to follow through on our
good intentions to listen and stay calm. Instead, we
react, strike back, go down the familiar road.

And there will be those moments. Conflict and emotional turmoil are an inescapable part of human life.
Within any partnership, family, work group, or society,
there is friction—the clash of our individual desires,

group ambitions, or cultural norms. We are left with the only thing we can control: choosing our response. Effective or ineffective.

Mastering "skillful means"—the art of negotiating differences, exchanging ideas successfully, cooperating creatively, and treating each other with kindness—is indeed a lifelong task. Relationships test us and stretch our humanity; not learning to exist in harmony with others carries a high price.

THE COST OF UNSKILLED CONFLICT

When we lack good relationship skills, troubles that could be quickly resolved morph into more difficult, harder-to-manage problems. Perhaps reflecting on our actions and reactions in times of conflict will cast light on the value of building these skills and incorporating them into our repertoire of habits. How we respond to moments of interpersonal tension really matters, in a number of important ways. Aside from reinforcing negative habits of reactive behavior, there are both long- and short-term consequences for our relationships.

My brother-in-law caught me on a good day. When he asked if I would sponsor his bike ride for Habitat for Humanity, I said sure and pledged forty-five dollars. A few weeks later, while on the road for business, I got his reminder e-mail. I meant to reply, but it got lost in the pile of things to do. By the end of the month, money was tight, so I didn't send the check. Instead, I wrote myself a note and forgot about it. Then, right in the middle of a big hassle at work, he called, saying the deadline was in a couple of days. I still didn't have the money and there were bills to pay. I was irritated that he'd bother me at the office. I snapped, "I'm really busy right now," and hung up. I couldn't admit that funds were short. I'm just a guy eking out a living and don't have time to go on two-week charity bike rides. Unlike him.

Trying to decide what to do, I got to thinking about how I never really liked him anyway. He only calls when he wants something. What's he ever done for me? Nothing. Does he ever invite me to play a round of golf or go to a ball game? No way. I ought to give him a piece of my mind.

So I did. I sent an e-mail: "You are such an ass," I wrote, thinking of that stupid grin he always has plastered on his face. "How dare you harass me for this money. It was a sad day when my sister married you. You know, I'm not going to contribute after all. You've never even tried to be part of the family, you smug S.O.B."

It felt great for a few days afterward. I really got some things off my chest. But my wife said she wished I hadn't done it. I got a very civilized note back saying, "Of course you can give or not give as you choose," and wishing me a good summer. I started to have some regrets. I guess he'd never been unkind to me, just reserved. We haven't spoken since, and it's been many months. I'm too uncomfortable, and embarrassed, to make the first move.

When we unload frustration in a single, fly-off-the-handle eruption, we may feel better initially. Upon reflection, however, we realize that unleashing our emotions did little to change the situation that brought about the outburst in the first place. In fact, it may have made it worse. We may proclaim that we simply "tell it like it is," but in doing so we bludgeon others and further damage our relationships.

After many years together, the initial romantic glow had cooled to an ember of warm constancy. The couple liked each other and, on the surface, got along famously. But they never really talked. They had it worked out on an unspoken level and kept their relationship amiable by avoiding controversial topics. "Talking about the relationship is the death of it," he would say. "When all we can do is talk about us, it means we have nothing left to say to each other." So they kept caring for each other, each harboring unspoken—even unknown—needs, quietly drifting . . . farther and farther apart. A crisis erupted when she was offered an exciting new job in another state, a chance at a new and different life. They couldn't negotiate this "sudden" problem. She moved away. He was left with an empty heart that ached, something he couldn't explain, even to himself.

On the other hand, we may decide not to speak our mind about a particular issue. In the short term, peace is preserved, but the long-term consequences are often hidden resentment and missed opportunities for real, meaningful exchange.

BUILDING SKILL IN RELATIONSHIPS

Truly engaging with others requires the sum total of all that we have learned. Over the centuries, many teachers have counseled us to use "skillful means" in our relationships, to seek harmony with others. Gautama Buddha's words on loving-kindness[2] outline the basic tenets of this approach:

This is what should be done
By those who are skilled in goodness,
And those who know the path of peace:
Let them be able and upright,
Straightforward and gentle in speech.

Although the prescription offered here seems uncomplicated, it is easy to misconstrue and—once understood—challenging to apply. A closer examination may help us clear away some common misconceptions about what it means to be skilled in this way.

Being "able and upright" implies placing our needs and the needs of others on an equal footing. To do this, we must know ourselves *and* empathize with others. When we realize the importance of this delicate and precarious balance, we will also see that being "straightforward and gentle in speech" is not just passive acceptance or giving in. It does not suggest we become a doormat for other people's mud, enduring mistreatment for the sake of harmony. There are times when we sacrifice for people we love, but we must be able to draw a clear line between giving *of* ourselves and giving *at the expense of* ourselves. Repressing our feelings or consistently yielding to another person's desires can breed depression, resentment, and illness.

Her husband expected too much. He had a well-paid "power job," while she was "just" a health professional. Over their ten years of marriage, she had taken on more and more of his day-to-day chores—buying his preferred brand of silk boxers, driving him to work, managing his calendar, ironing his shirts. He was a busy executive. She was ragged and spent. When she confronted him

*about taking care of his own personal errands, he didn't
get angry or even reply—he pouted and sulked for days.
She was furious but started taking care of his little
chores again, just to "keep the peace." Her migraines got
worse.*

Nor should being able, upright, straightforward, and
gentle be confused with clever manipulation. Flattering
the boss, being duplicitous, or knowingly manipulating
someone close to us is not the true sense of "skillful
means"; it is the underbelly of tuning in to others. How
tempting, how easy it can be to push the buttons and pull
the strings of someone we know very well, purring or
ingratiating to get what we want. A colleague and a seasoned veteran in marriage and family therapy says, "If
you've been together with someone for ten years or more,
you *really* know where their buttons are and how to push
them. You always *know*, you don't even have to think
about it." Conscious or unconscious manipulation makes
our relationships very complicated, even treacherous.

Because occasional conflict is necessary to maintain
long-term intimacy and cooperation, practicing loving-
kindness seeks to inform conflict in a constructive way.
Our task is to recognize the necessity of confrontation
and kindly and skillfully *engage in it*. And not just occasionally.

BEING UPRIGHT: THE BALANCE POINT
BETWEEN STRAIGHTFORWARD
AND GENTLE

Teachers in the East describe the difficulties with
standing upright in terms of "leaning in" and "leaning

back." An aggressive stance, "leaning in" results from being too attached to getting our way. It can show itself in fits of rage, where we unload our anger on others; excessive anxiety, where we become engulfed in fears; or severe self-criticism, where we scrutinize our every act. When leaning in, we hold too tight, push too hard, take small things too personally.

"Leaning back," on the other hand, stems from aversion. We observe life from a distance, rarely embracing passion, vigor, or active participation in our life. We shield ourselves from hurt, pain, loss, and disappointment—avoiding the "messiness" of inevitable conflicts and struggles with others. These defenses may indeed protect us, but at the cost of disengagement from others and ourselves.

By not leaning in or back, we stand "upright," meeting what life offers—sorrow, joy, failure, success, disappointment, surprise. We engage with others, acknowledge our interbeing, and allow our feelings to arise without backing away. With an easy confidence, we can consider, feel, and touch the experiences of others—although sometimes vastly different from our own—and yet maintain our individuality and personal integrity.

KIND SPEECH

> Sometimes a whisper is sufficient; at another time a shout may be best.
>
> JOHN DAIDO LOORI[3]

The agent of balance is kind speech—both in *what* we say and in *how* we say it. In the words of Dainin Katagiri-roshi, kind speech "can appear in various ways, but whatever kindness appears in our speech, we should remember that it must constantly be based on compassion or deep love. Under all circumstances that compassion is always giving somebody support or a chance to grow."[4] Here, he points out the importance of our intention as well as our words.

Sometimes kind speech is a soft whisper, supporting gesture, or gentle consolation. At other times, a shout may be necessary. We may need to assert our needs, set limits with a difficult person, or confront wrongdoing. Kind speech is more than just "nice talk." It involves disagreement without attack and honesty without judgment.

Confronting in the true sense of the word—a face-to-face exchange—is forthright, devoid of nastiness or aggression. We neither blame others for our discontent, nor demand that they satisfy all our emotional needs. Instead, we straightforwardly communicate our desires. Rather than expecting another person to pick up on subtle cues or "read between the lines," *we* bear the responsibility to articulate our views.

Our words—the seeds of beneficial action—are only a part of any interaction. More than just our words, kind speech involves our whole being—body language, demeanor, and delivery. Our intention is to help, not harm: "If we use rough language and scold someone, *it is necessary that it be based on very deep compassion. If we* forget, rough language really becomes rough language, hurting people"(italics mine).[5]

After laboring over his senior thesis, he sat on pins and needles, watching the professor read, nod, squint, and mark the paper casually with a red pen. When the pro-

fessor finished the silent critique, he looked up, straight at his student, took off his glasses, and calmly stated in a West Texas drawl, "This . . . is bullshit."

Taken aback, the student leaned forward to listen as the professor gently offered advice: "This isn't written from here," he said, patting his stomach. "Or here," tapping his chest. "Write what you think, what you believe. It's in there somewhere."

The student wrote a completely new paper and was later honored with the department's top prize. Now a professional writer, he remembers the moment fondly. "That professor was one of the most important influences on my career," he says. "I am—to this day—thankful for that moment of candor and kindness."

THE BENEFITS OF CARING

When we practice being able, upright, straightforward, and gentle, it can be contagious: "Kind speech is the basis for reconciling rulers and subduing enemies. Those who hear kind speech from you have a delighted expression and a joyful mind. Those who hear of your kind speech will be deeply touched—they will never forget it."[6]

Emanating from a single person, kind speech is the exponentially reflecting glint of each jewel, the melody of interbeing lingering like birdsong at dawn. In 1981, a study done by Howard Friedman and Ronald Riggio at the University of California, Riverside "found that . . . when three strangers sit facing one another in silence for a minute or two, the one who is most emotionally expressive transmits his mood to the other two—without a single word being spoken." Researchers have demonstrated repeatedly "how emotions spread irresistibly . . . whenever people are near one another."[7]

If we transmit good feelings outward, others will feel them. In fact, recent studies show that we transmit moods back and forth with others every day. Goleman, Boyatzis, and McKee report that "in 70 work teams across diverse industries members who were in meetings together ended up sharing moods—both good and bad—within two hours. . . . Groups, therefore, like individuals, ride emotional roller coasters, sharing everything from jealousy to angst to euphoria."[8] We have a choice. Whether at work, at home, or in public, we either catch other people's moods or inoculate them with ours. If we want to feel good, it helps to express goodness.

Gautama Buddha was precise about the benefits of kind speech. He said that intimacy and caring, as the force of loving-kindness, bring particular advantages: We will sleep easily and be filled with pleasant dreams. Waking, too, will be effortless. Our serene mind will show in a radiant countenance both expressing and attracting love, and, when death arrives, it will not be clouded in the confusion of a questionable life.

With emotional intelligence and years of practice, we can find the balancing point of compassion both for ourselves *and* for those whose paths we cross. On the way, missteps are unavoidable. But new habits open the gateway to harmony with others. This is how the ancients have counseled us to act. This is what we seek. And we must live it with our whole mind and body—a journey of thought, speech, and action. A journey whose implications reach far beyond each individual: "Kind speech . . . has the power to turn the destiny of the nation."[9]

SEEING THE EFFECT OF ANGER

Recent social research finds that anger is the mood people find the hardest to control.[10] "Indeed, anger is the most seductive of the negative emotions; the self-righteous inner monologue that propels it along fills the mind with the most convincing arguments for venting rage. Unlike sadness, anger is energizing, even exhilarating."[11]

University of Alabama psychologist Dolf Zillman conducted a series of studies recording what happens in the brain when we become angry,[12] offering new data on anger's mercurial nature. Amygdala hijacks, lack of sleep, and cumulative stress leave us edgy, primed and ready to overreact. Another stressor easily triggers another hijack. And, perhaps, *another* and *another.* Each successive angry thought becomes a mini trigger for the amygdala, sending additional surges of stress hormones through the body. Mini trigger after mini trigger, wave after wave of hormones, escalates the body's level of physiological arousal. Each angry feeling is far more intense than the one before. The emotional brain is on overload. We are swept up in a tsunami of hormone-induced anger. Flooded. Irrational. Out of control. "By then rage, unhampered by reason, easily erupts into violence."[13]

In my own upbringing, anger was a problem. I joke with my husband that I come from the "Loud Family," made up of Irish tempers; whoever yelled the loudest usually won the argument. The exception was my mother, who kept the peace and suffered from severe migraine headaches all her life. When my father drank, his outbursts of rage would sometimes deteriorate into violence. I grew up afraid of anger and vowed to keep my own at bay.

Consequently, I suppressed my angry feelings, swallowed down what bothered me, and concentrated instead on doing well in school. By my twenties, I had chronic migraine headaches and frequent stomachaches that later turned into a case of chronic colitis. In short, I was a physical and emotional mess by the age of twenty-four.

After my months in the monastery in Arizona and several years of counseling afterward, working on self-acceptance and forgiving my father's ills, I became more conscious of my anger and resentments. But once thawed, old bitterness sometimes erupted in red-hot rage. I shouted and slammed doors, "let it rip" when particularly provoked, and caused pain to those I loved.

Now solidly middle-aged, I claim "progress, not perfection" in this area. I notice flashes of anger sooner, catching them before harsh words fly. At this point, I am working with the more subtle layers of impatience, no longer victim of an "Irish temper" run rampant.

Anger, however, can be helpful in situations of mistreatment, abuse, or discrimination. In some circumstances, it acts as a catalyst for courage and prompts action. The challenge—even with well-founded anger—is to balance it with appropriate self-control and compassion for the other person(s) involved. Toward this end, I have found the following practice advocated by the Dalai Lama Tenzin Gyatso invaluable. Regarding the management of anger, he says:

> In the case of anger and hatred, although they arise naturally, in order to dispel or overcome them we have to make a conscious decision and deliberately cultivate their antidotes. . . . The idea is to stop it at an early stage, rather than wait for anger and hatred to arise

fully. Generally speaking, anger and hatred are the type
of emotions which, if left unchecked or unattended,
tend to compound themselves and keep on increasing.
The more one works with them, the more one adopts a
cautious attitude and tries to reduce the level of their
force, the better it is.[14]

The Dalai Lama draws the following visualization
from the eighth-century teachings of Shantideva in the
Guide to the Bodhisattva's Way of Life,[15] and instructs
us to contemplate the effects of irresponsible anger, on
others and ourselves.

We begin by imaging a picture of someone we know
losing his temper—seeing the mental agitation, physical
transformation, and harm caused to himself and others,
reflecting on the immediate effects of intense anger or
hatred. Because it can be easier to see the faults of others
than to admit our own flaws, we are instructed to imagine
someone else filled with anger and hatred.

After visualizing for a few minutes, we relate our
insights to our own experience and imagine suffering
similar consequences. We conclude the practice by
resolving never to let ourselves "fall under the sway of
such intense anger and hatred."

PRACTICE

 VISUALIZING THE EFFECTS OF
ANGER AND HATRED[16]

The Dalai Lama describes this practice as an analytical
meditation with a little bit of visualization. He says, "When
we think about these negative and destructive effects of

anger and hatred, we realize that it is necessary to distance ourselves from such emotional explosions."

WHAT YOU'LL NEED

- Twenty to thirty minutes to complete the practice.

- A quiet place to reflect and write.

- Your Personal Log.

TRY THIS

- Lie on your back or sit comfortably in a chair. Take a few moments to breathe. Feel your breath coming in and going out. Be aware of each in-breath and out-breath.

- After about three or four minutes, imagine a scenario where someone you know very well, someone who is close or dear to you, loses her temper—either in an acrimonious relationship or in a conflict situation.

- Imagine this person showing all the signs of an intense state of anger or hatred. See her losing her mental composure, creating negative vibes, even to the extent of harming herself and breaking things.

- Then pause to reflect on the effects of such intense anger or hatred. Picture how anger physically transforms her—no matter how hard she tries to stay dignified. Her face twists into an unpleasant expression. She sends out hostile vibrations like steam escaping her body—even her pets want to avoid her.

- Notice how this person you are fond of, whom you like, whose presence brought you pleasure in the past, now turns ugly—even physically.

- Hold this picture in your mind's eye, lingering to investigate the image for several minutes. These are the negative effects of generating anger and hatred.

- Take a few more moments, relating the image to your own experience of strong anger. Then resolve, *I shall never let myself fall under the sway of such intense anger and hatred. Because if I do, I will be in the same position and suffer all these consequences—lose my peace of mind, lose my composure, assume an ugly appearance, and so on.*

- Make that decision and develop a deep determination. Then relax, absorbing the insights of this meditation for several more minutes.

- After completing the meditation, take two or three minutes to reflect. Enter the date in your Personal Log and record your responses to these questions:

How did the person in my picture look?

_____

_____

_____

How did the person act? What was the person doing when angry?

_____

_____

_____

How did I feel toward the person in this mood state?

_____

_____

_____

*What consequences of anger and hatred do I want to avoid
incurring in my own life?*

_____

_____

_____

- Finish by writing out your intention—expressing
  your determination—to resist indulging in strong
  anger and hatred from this point forward. Refer to
  this intention in future moments when your "anger
  temperature" is rising.

Again and again we should try to counteract strong
anger and hatred, developing tolerance and patience
in their stead. When I need strength to do this, I think
of the following gatha, chanted by Cambodian monks
after the Killing Fields massacres:

*Hatred never ceases by hatred
But by love alone is healed
This is the timeless truth.*[17]

RESOLVING CONFLICTS WITH OTHERS

Although we cannot avoid the collision of individual
viewpoints and emotional triggers, we can handle these
situations as practices themselves. When viewed as practice, a conflict provides an opportunity to uncover and
become intimate with our own negative emotional
habits. This allows us to develop and enhance our communication skills. Facing conflicts opens us to more

compassionate interaction and frees us to live in greater
harmony, as any community must in order to address
the challenges that naturally arise between people.

OPENING TO A WORKING PAPER
ON CONFLICT RESOLUTION,
CLOUDS IN WATER ZEN CENTER,
ST. PAUL, MINNESOTA[18]

TURNING CONFLICT AROUND FOR THE BETTER

Adapted from a method for reconciliation that has
been used in monastic communities for thousands of
years, this practice emphasizes the Eastern notion of
taking "radical self-responsibility" when handling conflict. The version provided here, seasoned with insights
from Western psychology, currently serves the sangha
at Clouds in Water Zen Center. Although the original
techniques were designed to settle disputes within a
circle of monks, I think they are relevant and helpful
for families, churches, boards, corporations—the communities of the twenty-first century.

Here are three general suggestions for implementing
this practice in your day-to-day interactions:

1. *Examine your own mind before you speak.* Investigate the
   internal formations that spark your reaction. What is
   your intent here? What is your emotional agenda?
   (To win? To prove you are right? To establish blame?)
   Before you can approach another constructively, it
   helps to pause before reacting and temporarily suspend your emotional agenda. Only then is it possible
   to listen and have empathy. In order to feel *with*
   others, we need to move outside ourselves—without
   losing a sense of our own desires.

2. *Take radical responsibility for yourself in the conflict.* This includes owning your perspective, your inferences about the event, and the tone of your communication. We are not responsible for the actions of others. We are, however, responsible for skillfully asserting our needs. The distinction is framing our desires from the "I-position" (as in "I would appreciate it if you would not tell racist jokes at the dinner table") rather than from the demanding or accusing "You-position" (as in "You shouldn't show your ignorance by telling racist jokes at the dinner table"). Here, it is simply a clear articulation and dignified expression of *your* point of view.

Staying away from the word *you* helps prevent a nasty, hostile confrontation. Aggressive expression can take many forms, from sarcasm to disgust. Too often, we are unaware of how our sarcasm or disgust leaks through nonverbally. An exasperated sigh, a condescending roll of the eyes, or a contemptuous tone—an unspoken *you dummy* hanging in the air—is sure to trigger another's amygdala. Instantly. Instead, taking responsibility for our own needs and focusing on being upright in our communication can avoid provocation.

3. *Try to let go of the outcome.* An important element of being able to maintain your integrity during a conflict is what might be called "letting go of the outcome." When we articulate our wants, we are doing just that. Nothing more.

With the above explanations in mind, the following guiding principles from the conflict resolution model at Clouds in Water Zen Center can help us when resolving disagreements and misunderstandings with another:

In the midst of conflict, we believe it is important for each individual to:

- Take responsibility for our vulnerabilities and emotional triggers in relationships with others.

- Investigate our own responsibility in the conflict before speaking with another.

- Practice non-stubbornness by holding an open heart, a willingness to understand, and a desire to reconcile differences.

- Seek face-to-face resolution of the conflict with the other person or people involved.

- Use anger in a constructive and respectful way, allowing it to teach and transform us for the better.

- Separate the other person from his or her behavior, seeing the situation as an opportunity for personal learning and growth.

PRACTICE

 ## RESOLVING CONFLICT

The purpose of conflict resolution is to practice wisdom and compassion. This usually requires mutual understanding, forgiveness, problem solving, and learning from the situation in order to be more effective in the future. With this effort, resolving conflicts becomes practice itself.

CLOUDS IN WATER ZEN CENTER,
ST. PAUL, MINNESOTA

Step 1. *Before speaking with the other person, pause and reflect on your responsibility in the conflict.*

Think about these questions prior to discussing a conflict with another:

~ *What is my part in this conflict?* For example, *How have I been unskillful in this situation? What have I said or done or failed to say or do that has contributed to this conflict?*

~ *What triggered my emotional response? How am I feeling now? How is my own anger, jealousy, or fear driving my reaction?*

~ *What actions have led up to the current conflict? What do I remember about what led to the discord?* Look within to uncover your blind spots or selective memory.

~ *What do I think is going on? What is my perception or internal formation regarding this situation?*

Step 2. *Identify what you want to resolve the conflict and move on.*

Here focus on general wants—wishes, desires, and intentions—not specific actions. It can be either what you do want or what you don't want going forward.

Answer these questions in your Personal Log:

What do I want for myself regarding the issue?

_____

_____

_____

What do I want (that is positive) for the other individual involved?

_____

_____

_____

What do I want for our relationship?

_____

_____

_____

Step 3. *Discern what you need to say to the other person.*[19]

- Identify the root issues, what is most important to communicate.

- Make notes on what you need to say if the conflict is particularly heated.

- Clarify what you need in order to resolve the conflict, let go, and move on.

- Seek support from a friend, if needed, to go through the above steps.

Step 4. *Talk directly, face to face, with the other person.*

- Take full responsibility for your part in the misunderstanding, admitting your actions and their effect on the other person.

- Speak simply about your feelings and needs.

- Listen generously to the other person's feelings and needs—seeking to understand the issue(s) more deeply.

Step 5. *Generate solutions and agree on a new course of action, if needed.*
Think about and discuss:

~ *What would a successful outcome actually look like?* Picture it in your mind's eye and talk about it with the others present.

~ *What can I do to better the situation? Am I willing to apologize for my part in the situation, without making any attempt to justify myself or waiting for the other person to apologize first? Can I forgive the other person's lack of skillfulness and let go?*

~ *What will I do to better the situation? What actions am I willing to carry out? How can I change my own behavior going forward? Am I willing to improve my communication, refrain from unwanted behaviors? If so, how?*

A NOTE ABOUT MAKING AMENDS

Few things are as powerful as making amends for our words and actions—taking full responsibility for what we say and do, regardless of what triggered our response. It is a practice long advocated by twelve-step programs for recovering addicts and family members. Ironically, by taking full responsibility, we help ourselves as much as the other person. When we "own" our words and actions, we can do something about them. If we do not take responsibility, we are rendered powerless to change—it is someone else's fault, something else is to blame. We become a victim.

Here are a few things to consider when making amends:

- It is important to *say* something, to express your amends aloud. These beautiful words from Thich Nhat Hanh are an example: "I am sorry. I hurt you out of my lack of mindfulness, out of my lack of skillfulness. I will try to change myself."[20] Despite our best intention, there are times we hurt others. Although our intention is important, there is often a gap between our intention and the impact we have on others. All the components of upright and able, straightforward and kind speech are necessary to be effective.

- Making amends involves changing how we act. Just words are not enough. We need to make every effort to change our habits and actions for the better. Walking the walk not only lends credibility to our words but also forms new neural pathways, new habits of action. Speak your amends through your way of life.

SETTING LIMITS WITH A DIFFICULT PERSON

Therefore, just like any treasure appearing in my house
Without any effort on my part to obtain it
I should be happy to have a difficult person
For this difficult person assists me in my conduct of awakening.

SHANTIDEVA, EIGHTH CENTURY B.C.E.[21]

What if we try to resolve conflict with another to the best of our ability and it doesn't work—the other person is still difficult or even downright nasty? There *are* people who are aggressive, hostile, blaming, deceitful, or violent and likely to be defensive and in denial about their behavior. What then?

Over time, their relationship had gone downhill. When upset, her business partner would yell, fire off insults, and spew ugly accusations. At first these blowups were infrequent, but over the past several years they had become more persistent and out of control.

"I finally found an approach that seemed to work," she told me. "I would put my hand up and say Stop! *Then, after taking some deep breaths to steady myself, I would say, 'Could you speak slowly so I can understand you better? If you describe the problem to me slowly, I will try to listen. After you finish, I may have some questions.'"*

Emphasizing the use of the word slowly was important, she said. At first, she used the phrase Would you calm down? *but she discovered that it triggered more rage and usually escalated the conflict even further. Somehow, speaking slowly disrupted her partner's rage. But that was not the only benefit. "It eased the fear in me," she added. "It gave me time to focus on my breath and really try to tune in instead of reacting—getting angry, defending myself, or arguing back, as I had done so many times before. When I was calm enough to really try to listen, I had more clarity—I could see if she was being unreasonable. I felt less intimidated, because I was taking control of the situation by slowing it down. Too, I was able to have more compassion for her—despite how she acted."*

Sometimes her partner didn't stop raging when she put her hand up—she kept on . . . and on. "At first I would leave the office if she wouldn't stop, but then she would accuse me of running away. You bet I wanted to get away! But it gave her more to rage at me about. So, over time, I started to say, "I'm leaving now because this is not a constructive conversation. If you write down what you are concerned about and give it to me or e-mail it to

*me, I will read it and respond." Having a way to get out
of the situation physically was vital, she said. "It gave
me choices and helped me take better care of myself. After
going through this, I am not afraid of anyone—even a
bully." And as for her partner: "She learned her rages
had a consequence, that it was not okay for her to batter
me with her anger."*

Sometimes we may feel burdened, "done to," or helpless when dealing with a difficult person, adding more
hardship to an already painful situation. Or we can shift
our view about having such a person in our life—
embracing the "hidden treasure," learning memorable
and lasting lessons. If we allow it, the person can be a passage to increased depths of courage, control, or compassion—as a tough competition calls forth the best in an
athlete or performer. The ancient Shantideva advises us
to "be happy to have a difficult person" in our life, and
the modern Dalai Lama recommends we approach these
situations with gratitude. These are far more than
tongue-in-cheek comments: All of these highly developed spiritual teachers offer each one of us a very profound challenge.

On the other hand, "being happy" to learn from a
thorny situation does not suggest that we passively,
meekly, or piously accept whatever is done to us. There
are situations with difficult people that require clear
limits, even stern consequences—both to protect ourselves and our loved ones and, ultimately, to offer difficult people an opportunity to change for the better (if
they choose). The key is to be upright while presenting
our rights and needs, offering them without vengeance
or spite, with poise and respect. Consider this counsel
from the Dalai Lama:

Sometimes, you may encounter situations that require strong countermeasures. I believe, however, that you can take a strong stand and even take strong counter-measures out of a feeling of compassion, or a sense of concern for the other, rather than out of anger. One of the reasons . . . is that if you let it pass, then there is the danger of that person's habituating in a very negative way, which, in reality, will cause that individual's own downfall and is very destructive in the long run for the individual himself or herself. Therefore a strong coun-termeasure is necessary, but with this thought in mind, you can do it out of compassion and concern for the individual. . . . And, I think that countermeasures can ultimately be more effective without feelings of anger and hatred.[22]

When defining personal limits—how you let others treat you—it is important to realize it is not about attempting to control or change the *other* person. Per-sonal boundaries are about our own behavior. When our boundaries are loose or inconsistent, we let others intrude or allow them to mistreat us. If we don't set limits against emotional or physical abuse, *we* have become part of the problem. And we are not helping difficult people by allowing them to indulge in rages, deceit, or acts of harm. In fact, we may be making the situation worse.

We are responsible for taking care of ourselves. In fact, we are the expert on our own needs—we are the only one who can determine how we want to be treated, whom we are willing to spend time with, or if a question is too personal to answer. Our personal boundaries are more within our control than we may think. The fol-lowing practice will help you determine your limits and assert them with a difficult person.

PRACTICE

ASSERTING LIMITS WITH A DIFFICULT PERSON

If you have a difficult person in your life at home or at work, I recommend the following five steps as a way to determine your personal limits and the best course of action going forward.

WHAT YOU'LL NEED

- Quiet time to reflect—the amount of time needed to walk through these steps will vary from person to person. Working with this practice may take a few minutes, a few hours, or a few weeks, depending on the degree of difficulty in the situation you face and your readiness to take action.

- A good friend, counselor, or spiritual teacher to turn to for support.

- Your Personal Log.

TRY THIS

1. *First, review the actions you have taken to date.*
   Start by looking at how you have tried to handle your relationship with the difficult person—what you have said and done to this point. You may want to write out your last three encounters with the difficult person in your Personal Log and use it as the basis for this self-assessment. Take a moment to reflect on these questions:

~ What am I feeling about the relationship at this time—vengeful, afraid, exhausted, or calm?

_____

_____

~ How are my emotions affecting my response to the difficult person?

_____

_____

~ Am I repeating the same ineffective behaviors time and time again?

_____

_____

~ What's working and what isn't?

_____

_____

It is not unusual to become emotionally paralyzed when being mistreated—numb and unable to act effectively, hijacked by our amygdala. In this state, our bodies are so saturated with stress hormones that we can't think clearly. (Refer back to Signs of an Amygdala Hijacking in chapter 2.) Perhaps we haven't been able to see or follow through on an appropriate response—it may be that we haven't had a direct conversation with the difficult person about the behavior. Ask yourself:

~ Have I tried sitting face to face with the difficult person, making a sincere attempt to communicate the effect of his actions on me and asking him to change? Refer back to the Resolving Conflict practice earlier in this chapter.

~ If not, why not?

~ If so, have I made at least two or three efforts to talk, in different settings or at different times?

~ Do I see any other thing that a reasonable person could try to do that I haven't yet tried?

2. *Consider that you may be having trouble* accepting *the other person.*

Perhaps the problem doesn't only lie with the difficult person—you could be having a hard time accepting her. Maybe you don't want her to be the way she is, so—to buffer your feelings—you convince yourself otherwise. There can be many reasons for this, from your financial dependence on her to the amount of control she has over your personal or work life. Whatever the relationship, she is important to you. So it is more painful to accept her as she is.

You can test your acceptance by asking this question: *How many times have I said, "How could she have* done *that?"* If it is more than twice, it is likely that you are not seeing the other person completely or objectively. In this case, work on your acceptance of the difficult person *before* taking any action to set limits.

3. *Define your personal boundaries or limits for this situation.*
After working to accept the difficult person more fully, you are now in the state of mind to consider what personal boundaries or limits are necessary for you to stay in the relationship. Consider each of the following categories and determine your bottom line—what limits do you need to set about topics you are willing to discuss, time you can spend together, in what locations or settings? Think through your options now and make concrete plans for the next time you see the difficult person.

BOUNDARIES AROUND TOPICS

A client told me about her need to set limits around the "humor" during her family celebrations:

> *My uncle is a funny guy, warm and generous to a fault. And he harbors deep prejudice about people of color. After a few glasses of wine, he typically "entertains" the family with racist jokes, peppered with slurs and disparaging comments. My husband and I squirm and politely wait for the first chance to shift the conversation to a new topic. Sometimes we poke fun—hoping he gets the hint—but to no avail. We began to dread going to his house for dinner.*
>
> *My husband decided to talk with him one on one the next time we were together—before the drinking started. He said, "You are important to me and I want to have a good relationship with you. I think you are a great person. In that spirit, I need to tell you that I am uncomfortable when you tell racist jokes and belittle other people. I'd like to ask you not to do that from now on when we are together." It was an awkward and difficult exchange, but he took it well in the long run. Later that week, he called to tell my husband he appreciated his candor and would respect his request. He has never told a racist joke in our company since.*

Sometimes there are topics that are "sure trouble" if we get into them with the difficult person. Or there are topics that are private and off limits for all but certain intimate friends. Here, consider which issues you need to set limits around:

> ~ *Are there topics that are charged with emotion—subjects that usually cause trouble or trigger an amygdala hijack when I discuss them with the difficult person?*

~ Which of these subjects do I want to avoid in the future?

Once you have identified these "hot-button" topics, define how you want to limit your conversations in these areas in the future. Some examples are:

- I am uncomfortable discussing my parents' marital difficulties with either my mother or my father—it is not my business and it's too painful for me to hear about. I need to tell them both it's off limits for me.

- The next time she calls me and rages at me, I am going to say I won't talk with her when she is screaming at me but that I would really like to have a reasonable conversation about her concerns. If she persists, I will tell her I am willing to talk later—calmly—and hang up the phone.

- If he brings up my sex life again at work, I am going to change the subject or refuse to discuss it.

After determining the topics you want to avoid, move on to consider the limits you may need to establish around time. In a very volatile or destructive situation—when the difficult person is aggressive in criticism or demands—anyone can "lose it." In this case, it is important to admit our vulnerability and set limits around how much time we can spend with the difficult person.

BOUNDARIES AROUND TIME

In order to determine if you need to set limits around time, ask yourself:

~ *What is a reasonable amount of time to be with the difficult person? How long is it before the conversation typically deteriorates?*

~ *How can I limit my contact to this amount of time or less?*

~ *Within this time frame, if I start to get agitated or feel threatened, what can I do?*

~ *If the difficult person is getting agitated and the conversation is moving down the "same old familiar, negative path," what can I do?*

After reflecting, determine how much time you think you can spend with the difficult person and what you will do to extricate yourself if the situation begins to escalate. Some examples are:

- I can hold my own with him for about fifteen minutes—anything longer than that and it deteriorates into arguing or yelling. From now on, I am going to limit my conversations with him to fifteen minutes or less.

- It seems fine to visit with my mother for a few hours during the day, but staying for the weekend is usually trouble—next time I am going to get a hotel room in the neighborhood instead.

- I want to continue to see her, but only occasionally.

If you read early warning signs that the situation is about to escalate into raging, violence, or emotional harm, you can set personal boundaries by:[23]

- Suspending the conversation.
- Leaving the room and talking later when you are both calm.

- Refusing to read any further mail or e-mails from this person.

- Stopping the car or refusing to drive with the other person.

- Removing yourself and any children from the abusive situation.

Next, consider what boundaries you may need around settings or locations. At times, a particular setting or location can provide a "safety net" for contact with the difficult person—an environment that prevents unwanted touch, emotional outbursts, threats, or violence. Likewise, there may be places you want to avoid.

BOUNDARIES AROUND SETTINGS OR LOCATIONS

In order to determine if you need to set limits around physical settings or locations, ask yourself:

~ *In private, does my interaction with the difficult person often deteriorate to yelling, screaming, or physical threats?*

~ *Am I at risk of losing control of my own emotions, being carried away by anger or fear?*

~ *Am I in physical danger with this person?*

~ *What settings can provide a "safety net" for me when I need to meet with the difficult person?*

~ *How can I limit my contact to these settings or locations?*

Next, identify the specific settings or locations that are appropriate for meeting with the difficult person—and be prepared to follow through with your decision! Some examples are:

- I am only going to be with her when a third party is present.

- I won't go to bars with him.

- I will only meet with her in public places, like a restaurant or park.

- I will not attend business meetings that run until late into the evening.

- I am willing to spend time with him but not his spouse.

4. *Calmly and clearly assert your personal limits with the other person.*

Now that you have defined the limits you need to set, the next step is to talk with the other person about them. Before attempting this, clear yourself of anger or vengeance or spite so you can be calm and compassionate in your presentation. You may want to return to the Mountain Meditation or Circle of Protection practice in chapter 7, Staying Poised, to prepare yourself for the conversation. In addition, it may be useful to write out what you are going to say and practice it with a good friend beforehand.

When speaking face to face with the difficult person, be specific and communicate one limit at a time. At all costs, stay calm and matter-of-fact, even if the difficult person attempts to provoke you into conflict or old behavior. Expressing anger in this situation is counterproductive, so draw deeply upon your conviction and poise. If you find yourself losing control, stop, take a break, or physically leave with a promise to resume the conversation at another time or in another mode—by telephone, in writing, or with a third party present.

Finally, hold a firm and kind stand—persist if your limits aren't observed right away. Consistent follow-through is the only way to protect yourself *and* help the difficult person change for the better. You may want to seek out a friend, a therapist, or a spiritual teacher to support you in your resolve.

5. *Measure your success by the things you can control.*
In the end, we may or may not ever know the impact setting limits has on other people. They may or may not change. But *you* have changed and can respond to them in new ways. In *Stop Walking on Eggshells,*[24] Paul Mason and Randi Kreger suggest the following checklist for evaluating our "success" in setting limits with a difficult person. I think it is an excellent litmus test, buffering the feelings of failure we may experience when the other person keeps on their destructive ways. Here we view "success" from the perspective of what we *can* control—ourselves.

~ *Did I act in a way that demonstrated self-respect?*

~ *Was I clear about my position?*

~ *Did I stay calm and composed?*

~ *Did I remain focused, even if the difficult person tried to draw me off track?*

~ *Did I refuse to be baited and drawn into a losing argument?*

~ *Was I considerate of the other person's feelings, even if this person did not give the same consideration?*

~ Did I maintain a firm grip on my reality while maintaining an open mind toward the other person's concerns?

Then, too, if the difficult person refuses to respect your personal limits, you may need to face the question of whether or not you can have a relationship at all. You may need to keep distance from the difficult person for a period of time, leave your job, transfer positions, put an end to your business partnership, or stop seeing the person altogether. After all our effort, despite receiving the treasure of our personal growth, we may still experience loss and grief about our relationship with the difficult person, particularly a loved one.

A participant in one of my seminars on emotional intelligence sent me a letter with this description of letting go of a loved one she could not change:

She is my sister and will always be a part of me. But for now, I cannot spend time with her. My very presence seems to trigger her rage. The last time I saw her was at Christmas. She came for the get-together but wouldn't speak to me, looked through me as if I wasn't there. After the first hour, I calmly said, "I think it is very hurtful of you to refuse to talk to me and I don't appreciate being treated this way." She flew into a rage, screaming at me, coming up close and shaking her fist barely an inch from my face, saying, "You can't make me do anything, I'll act however I want and you can't stop me." My mother begged her not to spoil the holiday, my younger sister started crying, and her sons tugged on her to stop—but she simply turned her fury toward them instead. It was horrible.

She has been through years of therapy, a divorce, and cancer—even her medical doctors told her she needed to control her anger for the sake of her health. I have tried everything I know how to do to have a relationship with her—swallowing her mistreatment, talking, confronting her behavior, writing, calmly setting limits. And this is where we are at this point in time. For now, I keep up a relationship with her sons—my beloved nephews—but I don't try to communicate with her or see her.

All I can do is hold her in a circle of loving-kindness and pray for her well-being. I am able to do this better from afar, safely out of range from her hatred and meanness. At least it's something and I still hold hope that someday she will be better and we can connect again, like we used to when we were young.

TRAIL MARKER

Whew! These last steps were uphill, with a steep grade. Rest a while, breathing in the fragrance of the air, taking in the view.

Here you made use of all your abilities to nurture and maintain effective relationships—self-knowledge, poise, compassion, and skillful means. A spiritual life takes place in the world, interacting with others. Harmony is made of your words, your actions, your "conduct of awakening." It is both the end and beginning of all your efforts—the path to more peaceful living, the way to deeper wisdom.

And so, when you have done everything there is to do in a world beyond your control, we move to letting go.

CHAPTER 10

LETTING GO

All is flux; nothing stays still.

HERACLITUS[1]

We stand at the summit in this living moment of now with a clearer vision, a new point of view. Before us, behind us, around us, within us lies the labor of our climb—the pathways etched by the conscious effort of each step along the way.

From here we see the valley of cultivated awareness, where the roadway descended into the fettering knots and tangles that poison the mind. We greeted them as old friends, companions on the trail, in the sunlight of nonjudging acceptance.

We paused, gathering poise—a moment of stillness to consider our way—before continuing uphill. No longer blown about by our gusting moods, freed from undue doubt and fear, we can better choose our direction. We notice how the play of light from dawn to dark can affect the way we see. Using the compass of our awareness, we determine the remaining route into territory yet unknown.

On this new trail, reflected in the Jewel Web, we saw our own feelings in the faces of others on the road, breathing *with,* feeling *with,* talking *with*—connecting. Treading lightly here. Stepping firmly there. Around the jagged edges of conflict, we traveled on toward the heights of harmony, renewed by the climb. We did not turn back.

But from this point, we see that everything in view is not—artist's brush in hand—as we would have painted it. "Pleasure and pain, gain and loss, praise and blame, fame and disrepute constantly arise and pass away, beyond our control."[2] We cannot bend life to our own will; it is as it will be. Others, too, have their journey and their path. Despite our best efforts, there is failure, betrayal, illness, and loss. We are in control only of the steps we take and the choices we make.

Here we can surrender to an unchanging truth: that every moment is in motion, from the molecules we are made of to the distant edges of the universe. Billions of neurons sending signals, connecting, shaping and reshaping. The nature of life is impermanence. We can find peace here—knowing we have done all that we can, but still we must let go and . . .

> . . . *see this fleeting world*
> *A star at dawn,*
> *A bubble in a stream,*
> *A flash of lightning in the summer sky,*
> *A flickering lamp,*
> *A phantom and a dream.*[3]

We taste this impermanence. We breathe it. Feel the grief of it. Resist it. Protect ourselves against the inevitability of loss. It aches. Anger, bitterness, and frustration following in the wake. Waves of sadness and yearning for the way things were. Anxiety about a future unknown. Yet knowing, too, that there is a light beckoning us from the other side of grief. We have more steps to take—in the attitudes *we* hold, in *our* view of life, in the way *we* relate to others.

THE FOUR SUBLIME ATTITUDES

Our ancestors—meaning those who have gone before, suffered the same desires as you and I—offered these teachings on the Four Sublime Attitudes.[4] Said to foster enlightened emotions, increase inner peace, and reflect attributes of the divine, the attitudes counsel us to practice friendliness, compassion, gladness, and unshakable serenity.

FRIENDLINESS

The first sublime attitude calls us to hold friendliness and goodwill in our heart—toward *all people*. In the normal course of life, we "love" the people we are close to, the people we enjoy—our family, our friends, our lover, our colleagues, our community of like-minded people. Those outside our circle can be overlooked, distrusted, or disliked. By contrast, "friendliness" invites us to peek outside our cocoon of preoccupation or comfort and become aware of those around us. It speaks of an unselfish love.

I remember, after a year's project in Asia, being struck by the paucity of manners in the American culture—the simple, common practices of saying *please* and *thank you* when ordering a meal or receiving service in Japan. I made a personal decision to practice these courtesies in everyday interactions and am surprised at the attention and effort it continues to require.

Friendliness toward others begins with the self. If our minds are filled with harshness, worry, or envy, it is nearly impossible to be open with others. A friendly attitude requires a warm, charitable heart.

We can cultivate generosity with an ancient Eastern practice called *Metta,* the giving and receiving of loving-kindness. It instructs us to meditate on our *own* well-being by silently repeating thoughts such as *May I be well. May I be free from ill feeling and troubled thoughts. May I be filled with loving-kindness. May I be filled with joy. May I be at peace and at ease. May I live happily.* These phrases, when repeated in a "slow, graceful, purposeful way"[5] gradually penetrate our mind and heart, creating new neural pathways to replace old knots of anger, craving, and fear. We literally have something new to think about.

Over time, *Metta* practice shapes our everyday interactions and makes room for the needs of those close to us. This friendliness then expands outward toward others, and saying hello or offering a smile to strangers becomes an expression of genuine affection. As we mature in this practice, we can even empathize with those we dislike or consider enemies until our concerns reach far beyond our own well-being to include the "peace, harmony, goodwill, and welfare of all living beings."[6]

With the thought *May I live happily,* we begin to expand our generosity outward, making room in our hearts for those we hold dear, then to others we do not know, and, finally, as we deepen in our maturity, to those we dislike or consider enemies. Fostering friendliness—being concerned for the "peace, harmony, goodwill and welfare of all living beings"[7]—can displace thoughts of anger, dislike, or spite. It gives us something else to think about, a new neural path to travel, besides what concerns only *me*.

COMPASSION

The second sublime attitude, compassion, builds on friendliness. Not only are we able to hold hope for the well-being of others, but we also suffer with them. We empathize with their struggles without absorbing their pain to the point that it overwhelms us. We can be of little help if we take over the responsibility for another person's happiness. As we saw in the practice Asserting Limits with a Difficult Person, true empathy means we *care for* rather than *take care of* other people. In the end, we can only be responsible for compassionate assistance—respecting the other person's life choices.

Compassion puts a dent in self-absorption. Yet it can best be developed from the seeds of our own suffering. Byakuren Judith Ragir, a Zen priest in Minnesota and former student of the late Dainin Katigiri-roshi, offers this suggestion for developing our compassion. "When experiencing a difficulty or painful circumstance, ask yourself how many other people in your neighborhood, your city, your country, or in the larger world are experiencing something similar right now, in this moment." It might go something like this:

~ *How many other people have lost their jobs today?*

~ *How many others have had to start over?*

~ *How many others went to sleep last night worrying about losing their homes?*

~ *How many others are scared?*

~ *How many others are lonely?*

~ *How many others think they are the only ones with difficulties like these?*

This simple practice can lift us out of self-pity, out of isolation, out of our small world. It can open our heart to knowing others suffer, too; suffer now in similar, perhaps graver, ways. Compassion is medicine for cruelty in the world. A compassionate stance prompts us to act—to show kindness, to give aid where possible, to

help others in need—when in the past we were too busy
or didn't realize it mattered.

GLADNESS

The next sublime attitude, gladness, shines through the
whole range of human experience, humor and tragedy,
victory and defeat. We hold this attitude when we gen-
uinely delight in the success and happiness of others.
Gladness also means maintaining a joyful mind—
grateful and buoyant—through hardship and loss. I
know personally just how difficult this is. Last summer,
I was reminded how much my mother, with her words
and actions, is still teaching me the art of grace and
how to live with dignity.

Amid the fireworks and fanfare of the Fourth of July,
I knew something was terribly wrong. As the weekend
began, she was reading, watching TV, and driving as she
had always done—managing well with only one "good"
eye. But by the end of the holiday weekend, she could
see only through the edges of her peripheral vision.
The world she had known—of colors and shapes, faces
and sky—became nothing but shifting shadows and
vague light. According to the doctor, her condition
("wet" macular degeneration) causes veins to leak into
the eye. After several laser surgeries failed to remedy
the problem, any hope that she would recover her sight
was lost. She was declared legally blind. I was sure this
would plunge her into depression and bitterness, but
perhaps these thoughts were merely projections of how
I would feel if I lost my sight.

Instead my elderly mother handled it with bravery
and grace. After six months, she seemed more content
than I had ever known her—cheery and uncannily intu-

itive. At dinner one evening, I said, "This may seem like a strange thing to say, Mother, but you seem happier since you went blind. How can that be?"

"It's not that I am happier," she replied. "I really miss being able to see. There are certainly times when I am frustrated and angry about it. Other times, I want to cry. But you know, so many people have been kind and helpful, I feel like I have angels in my life." She paused. "I have learned to think more about what I have in my life than what I don't have . . . every day I try to spend time being grateful, thanking God for my many blessings."

A heart of gladness embraces the people and events in our lives—the triumphs and sorrows. When the tide rises, we rejoice in good fortune, delighting in the talents and blessings of our loved ones. When it ebbs, we search for meaning, giving thanks for the gifts we have already been given. Gladness is accepting what we *have,* knowing that "a person who develops gladness attracts many friends and lives with others in harmony."[8] It counteracts our very human tendencies toward envy, jealousy, and self-pity. Instead we are rich in contentment. As the tides of fate rise and fall, we have little choice in the matter. In response, we can choose gladness or bitterness. Why not choose gladness?

UNSHAKABLE SERENITY

> If you can do something about it, why worry? If you can't do anything about it, why worry?
>
> SHANTIDEVA[9]

The last of the sublime attitudes, unshakable serenity, is the most advanced and difficult of all. Also referred to as equanimity, it incorporates the warmheartedness of the previous three attitudes (friendliness, compassion, and gladness) but it "also has balance, wisdom, and the understanding that things are as they are, and that we cannot ultimately control someone else's happiness and unhappiness."[10]

Unshakable serenity provides quiet power, the wisdom to know the difference between what we can and cannot change, however much we may desire it. Rather than becoming immobilized with anxiety, frustration, or despair over things beyond our control, we can learn to meet them with loving courage. Although we still grieve, we can disengage from useless fretting, meddling, or enabling, and better meet difficult situations with undisturbed peace of mind.

Equanimity requires that we let go of quick judgments about what is "good" or "bad." This ancient Chinese folktale[11] reminds us to be patient—to wait and see how things will turn out:

> There is a Taoist story of an old farmer who had worked his crops for many years. One day his horse ran away. Upon hearing the news, his neighbors came to visit. "Such bad luck," they said sympathetically. "Maybe—who knows what's good or bad," the farmer replied. The next morning the horse returned, bringing with it three other wild horses. "How wonderful," the neighbors exclaimed. "Maybe—who knows what's good or bad," replied the old man. The following day, his son tried to ride one of the untamed horses, was thrown, and broke his leg. The neighbors again came to offer their sympathy on his misfortune. "Maybe—who knows what's good or bad," answered the farmer. The day after, military officials came to the village to draft young men into the army. Seeing that the son's leg was broken, they

passed him by. The neighbors congratulated the farmer on how well things had turned out. "Maybe," said the farmer, "who knows what's good or bad."

As in the story, suspending our judgment—keeping an open, *I-don't-know-yet* mind—allows new perspectives to enter into our awareness. We patiently wait to see what will come. Grieve losses in the moment. Consider outcomes not yet imagined. Release the heart to wider spaces. Carry the hope of human promise. This is the gift of equanimity.

Ancient teachers tell us to practice these attitudes until they are ingrained in our mind and absorbed by our heart. Although they didn't call it *etching new pathways in the brain,* they simply knew from experience that this was the course to personal transformation.

When all is said and done, we have only each moment and our choices—what attitudes to hold, what steps to take, what paths to walk, what legacy to leave. In the words of an ancient Eastern adage: "My deeds are my closest companions. I am the beneficiary of my deeds. My deeds are the ground on which I stand."[12] The practice of equanimity will help us shape our deeds with calm consideration, with heart and mind engaged, with greater wisdom.

USING EQUANIMITY PHRASES TO LET GO

Meditating with equanimity phrases can be consoling when faced with a relationship or circumstances beyond our control—freeing us to let go. In the ancient teachings, equanimity permeates loving-kindness, compassion, and gladness, grounding them with a sense of "patience, that ability to be constant and endure, even if the love, sympathy or rejoicing is unreturned, even through all the ups and downs."[13]

Practicing equanimity sows unshakable serenity—stilling our mind and heart and etching new pathways to counteract agitation, worry, and the sorrow of loss. Here we learn to weather the ills of life and the pain of disappointment with greater resiliency and inner peace. By training our mind—reshaping our brain—we become tranquil and composed, moved but unmoving. Serene.

In this state, we can see things closer to how they really are—grander than our own desires, beyond our ability to understand, larger than our own small world. Greater serenity allows us to open our mind to new possibilities, to consider thinking, *Maybe! Who knows what's good or bad?* in the face of failure or disappointment.

Accepting other people or circumstances *as they are* gives us peace. We still do all that we can to change things for the better. But all the while, we practice letting go of what we cannot control. It's either that or madness.

PRACTICE

 MEDITATING WITH EQUANIMITY PHRASES[14]

Repeating equanimity phrases during sitting meditation is a form of *Metta* practice—a way to cultivate calmness of mind and kindness of heart. I have adapted this practice by weaving in threads from the Judeo-Christian traditions.

In Western thought, this practice could be considered a "nondirected prayer strategy"—as opposed to a directed method, where we ask for specific outcomes. Here we do not inflict our personal wishes on another. We simply ask, in general terms, for their well-being. A number of studies, reported by Larry Dossey in *Prayer Is Good Medicine*,[15] show that nondirected and directed prayer are equally effective.

When beginning, think of someone you can feel for easily. Spend time learning the practice and training the mind in equanimity. If you develop this emotional habit when facing a mildly difficult situation, it will be there for you when you are in great need. So begin with this "easy person" and then progress to more difficult people or situations—with friends, family, and, ultimately, those you consider enemies.

WHAT YOU'LL NEED

• Fifteen to twenty minutes of undisturbed time.

• A quiet place to sit or lie down.

• Your Personal Log.

TRY THIS

• Take the first five minutes to breathe mindfully. Assume a comfortable position, breathe easily, and keep an alert mind, sitting so that your body is relaxed and your spine is straight. Feel your breath come in and go out, in and out. Keep full awareness on the in-breath, full awareness on the out-breath . . . then start the practice.

   (If you are in an agitated state of anger, worry, or concern, you may want to spend a longer time calming yourself before you start the meditation. If this is the case, consider returning to the Mountain Meditation in chapter 7, Staying Poised, soothing and stilling yourself before you begin working with the equanimity phrases.)

• Begin by calling to mind the person or situation that needs letting go. Start by working with your own distress and agitation. Draw a Circle of Protection (see chapter 7, Staying Poised) around yourself, encircling yourself with the white light of happiness and kind understanding. Maintain this image for several minutes, breathing in the energy of compassion, breathing out any grief or pain you are carrying.

• Then gently recite an equanimity phrase such as:

  ~ *May I accept* [say the name of the person] *as he/she is.*

  ~ *May I be undisturbed by the comings and goings of events.*

• Next, send out white light rays to the person you are holding in meditation. Surround him with the warmth of compassion. Emanating from your heart, it touches him and transforms him according to his personal need at the moment he receives it. Make a strong wish for his suffering to be removed, for any and all emotional distress to be consoled.

• While holding a sense of this person in your mind, softly recite an equanimity phrase several times—even a hundred times, or more—offering each word with love. The traditional phrases in *Metta* practice are:

All beings are the owners of their karma. Their happiness and unhappiness depend on their actions, not upon my wishes for them.

You can use these prayers or phrases, or create your own, fitting your beliefs and tradition, such as:

~ [Name the person]—*I will care for you but cannot keep you from suffering.*

~ [Name the person]—*I wish you happiness but cannot make your choices for you.*

- If you start to feel yourself drifting into impassiveness, reflect on the fact that equanimity can bring you courage to face adversity. Reflect on the vastness of change and how many things are outside your control. Sharpen your focus on the person or group you are directing equanimity to, then go back to repeating the equanimity phrases.[16]

- Next, release the entire situation, turning it over to a Power Greater than Yourself (God, Christ, Buddha, the Great Mystery of Life . . .). Repeat a phrase such as:

~ *May the best outcome prevail.*

~ *May the highest good be obtained.*

~ *May Thy will be done.*

Or you may wish to recite the Serenity Prayer:

God, grant me the serenity to accept the things I cannot change, the courage to change the things that I can, and the wisdom to know the difference.

- Close the meditation by holding general thoughts of goodwill toward all living beings in the ten directions. With the out-breath, exhale white light, originating in your heart, flooding the entire space around you, washing over every living being. Do this for several moments, slowly repeating in your mind:

May all living beings
Be free from animosity,
Free from oppression,
Free from trouble,
May they look after themselves with ease.[17]

- Finally, allow a moment of silence and stillness before getting up. Slowly move your hands and feet; feel the wholeness of your body again before returning to your day's routine. (If you wish, pause and write down key insights from this meditation in your Personal Log or in the space below.)

This practice leads to a deep feeling of well-being. Barriers between ourselves and others can be broken, and we can find our way to unshakable serenity.

PARTING WORDS

In this book, you have been introduced to a sampling of collective wisdom gathered from the past and present. You have learned a new way to think about how the brain works—how the limbic system governs our emotional reactions, and how the thinking brain can inspire more positive actions, in the present moment and for the future.

Realizing that your reactions are rooted in the deeply ingrained neuropathways of your emotional habits, you can take control and change them for the better. For yourself. For others. With a deep retooling at the neurological level, you can re-form your emotional habits, break new trails in the brain and in your life. This process of change parallels any journey into new territory, not unlike trekking to the peak of Kanchenjunga—my own sojourn to the heart of the Himalayas in Sikkim. It requires great determination, consistent effort, and the support of others.

Guiding us on the path are ancient practices handed down for generations. These are practices used to shape the lives of those whose footsteps we follow, real people with struggles and triumphs much like our own. They leave us with their hard-won wisdom, born from experience and tested through the years. Their gift is a road map to inner transformation and unshakable serenity.

They tell us to live mindfully, to notice the rhythm of our breathing, to heed the language of our body. They encourage us to experience the broad and colorful range of human emotions by investigating root causes and unraveling mental knots. Then we cultivate poise. We ponder the still strength of the mountain and absorb its resolute calm. We see the scars left by undue anger and hatred and vow to find the way to harmony with others. We are, after all, of the same substance, woven together in Indra's Net.

At last, we turn to the sublime attitudes of friendliness, gladness, gratitude, and equanimity. These are the pathways we seek to etch in the brain, and these are the practices that lead us to that end. They have enriched my own life and the lives of colleagues, clients, and friends around the world.

I offer them to you with the hope that you will use this book until it is tattered and worn, guiding your mind, opening your heart, and shaping the pathways of your brain into what *you* want them to be. Although what we ultimately desire is a vibrant, vivid life, it is in the practice—the walking—that we attain serenity and find the path. Remembering that "there is no path . . . paths are made by walking."[1]

Looking back, we see the way. We realize that "the road up and the road down is the same,"[2] and *this* is the mystery of the path—a circle, a spiral, an unending journey from self through others back to self, and so on . . . in the quest for deeper wisdom and greater love.

May your journey be one of joy.

APPENDIX

Examples of Wisdom Figures from a Variety of Religious Traditions and Modern Culture

Archetype = Wisdom

Buddhism[1]	Judaism[2]	Christianity[3]	Indigenous Peoples[4]	Modern Culture
MANJUSRI	SOLOMON, KING OF JUDEA	THE HOLY SPIRIT, THE PARACLETE	THE TEACHER (WEST)	ALBERT EINSTEIN BOB DYLAN GERTRUDE STEIN
He is often depicted as a young man, riding a lion and holding a sword in his right hand, symbolizing his ability to see and penetrate the essence of all things. His youthfulness depicts a childlike clarity available to all, regardless of age.	The son of David and Bathsheba, Solomon is described as "wiser than all men." Hoping to be a benevolent and judicious ruler, he prayed for a "listening heart" and "understanding mind." In the case of the two women each claiming the same child as her own, his order to "cut the child in two" revealed the child's true mother.	Depicted as a tongue of fire or the wind, the Holy Spirit is referred to as the "life-giving breath of God" in both the Old and New Testaments. A source of strength and wisdom, the Holy Spirit has been a force of discernment and counsel for prophets, leaders, and miracle workers throughout time.	Ancient peoples used nautical creatures to portray wisdom, often depicting them sitting in still silence. In indigenous traditions, a wise, insightful teacher is often associated with the direction of west, the season of autumn, and the element of water.	

Archetype = Compassion

AVALOKITESHVARA	RUTH, GREAT-GRANDMOTHER OF DAVID	MARY, MOTHER OF JESUS	THE HEALER (SOUTH)	DALAI LAMA MOTHER TERESA ALBERT SCHWEITZER
According to legend, she was about to enter heaven but paused on the threshold as the cries of the world reached her ears. She is often depicted with a thousand arms, sometimes with an eye in the palm of each hand, seeing and sensing the afflictions of humanity. She embodies the omnipresent mother.	The daughter-in-law of the widow Naomi, Ruth is known for her kindness and patience. Often consoling the depressed and bitter Naomi, she exemplifies true friendship, support, and unconditional love.	Born in Jerusalem and betrothed at the age of fourteen, Mary is revered as a holy and virtuous woman, the perfect mother, and an intercessor between human beings and God. She is said to know the deepest of human suffering, having borne witness to the agonizing and humiliating death of her son, Jesus. She is sometimes depicted with swords piercing her heart, a sign of her great compassion.	In the ancient Medicine Wheel, compassion figures are usually depicted as four-legged creatures. Often portrayed telling stories, they are seen as healers. A compassion figure is associated with the direction of south, the season of spring, and the element of earth.	

Archetype = Action

SAMANTABHADRA	ESTHER, QUEEN OF PERSIA	JESUS OF NAZARETH, SON OF GOD	THE WARRIOR (NORTH)	MARTIN LUTHER KING JR. / MAHATMA GANDHI / AUNG SAN SUU KYI
She is often depicted on a white elephant, representing calm, deliberate activity imbued with careful intention and dignity. She represents the expression of wisdom and ethical conduct in the real world.	This Jewish queen risked her position and her life to save the Jews from persecution and death. The entire Book of Esther is a story about her initiative: She breaks the law to risk approaching the king unbidden and arranges two public banquets to expose the evil of Haman, a member of the king's court.	Born in Galilee, he is believed to be "the Christ"—Son of God, healer, teacher, and radical reformer. His teachings demanded a response of the whole person and not merely the observance of the religious laws of the times.	The action figure is seen as a warrior by land-based peoples and is often depicted dancing. Action-warriors are usually symbolized as winged creatures. They are associated with the direction of north, the season of winter, and the element of air.	

Archetype = Empowerment

MAHASTHAMA-PRAPTA	DANIEL THE PROPHET	LYDIA, THE MACEDONIAN DISCIPLE	THE VISIONARY (EAST)	MAYA ANGELOU NELSON MANDELA VACLAV HAVEL
He is the bodhisattva of strength and enlightened power. He overcomes all outer and inner obstacles. He is depicted as standing erect and having a pagoda ornament in his hair.	A pious Jewish youth, Daniel was deported to Babylon by King Nebuchadnezzar. He matured into a seer capable of interpreting the king's dreams and receiving visions for the future. Cast into a lion's den because he refused to give up his faith, Daniel remained "unhurt because of his trust in God."	A resident of Thyatira, Lydia was a successful dealer in purple-dyed goods and head of a sizable household when she met Paul the apostle. She converted to Christianity and led missionary efforts in the region, moving beyond the acceptable bounds for women of that era.	An empowered figure is seen as a visionary by land-based peoples and often depicted as singing. Desert land and no-legged creatures usually symbolize visionaries. They are associated with the direction of east, the season of summer, and the element of fire.	

NOTES

[1]Antonio Machado, *Proverbios y Cantares* (Proverbs and Songs), 29 in *Selected Poems of Antonio Machado,* translated by Betty Jean Craige, University of Georgia (Baton Rouge: Louisiana State University Press, 1979). Antonio Machado (1875–1939) was a Spanish poet, essayist, and dramatist.

PART ONE: BREAKING TRAIL
CHAPTER 1: THE PATH

[1]Pablo Neruda, *Toward the Splendid City,* upon receiving the Nobel Prize.

CHAPTER 2: THE SCIENCE OF EMOTIONS

[1]Robert Ornstein, *The Evolution of Consciousness: The Origins of the Way We Think* (New York: Simon & Schuster, 1991).

[2]These signs of an amygdala hijack are adapted from Daniel Goleman, *Emotional Intelligence* (New York: Bantam Books, 1995).

[3]Describing activity of neurotransmitters in the brain as "kind of like scrubbing bubbles" is from R. M. Restak, *Brainscapes* (New York: Hyperion, 1995).

[4]Gerald Edelman, *Neural Darwinism: The Theory of Neuronal Group Selection* (New York: Basic Books, 1987).

[5]Joseph LeDoux, *The Emotional Brain* (New York: Touchstone Books, 1996).

[6]The inhibitory action of neuron: Daniel Goleman, *op. cit.*

[7]Role of the prefrontal lobe during stress: Daniel Goleman, *op. cit.*

[8]The effect of mindfulness meditation on the brain: Daniel Goleman, *op. cit.*

[9]Brain changes at Promega were measured by the state-of-the-art method, a functional MRI before, and after training. Those who went through the training were compared with a random control group of peers who had not yet had the training. The data was collected by Richard Davidson, director of the Laboratory for Affective Neuroscience at the University of Wisconsin. From Daniel Goleman, *op. cit.*

[10]*Sutra* is the word for Buddhist scripture, referring to the direct words and teachings of the Buddha in 500 B.C.E.

[11]Three versions of the Sutra on the Four Establishments of Mindfulness have come down to us over the centuries. The reference in this book is from a first-century B.C.E. scripture of the Theravāda school of Buddhism, recognized as version 1 of the Sutra. The edition quoted here is from the Pali Satipatthana Sutra (number 10 in the Majjhima Nikāya), translated by Thich Nhat Hanh and Annabel Laity in *Transformation and Healing, Sutra on the Four Establishments of Mindfulness* (Berkeley, CA: Parallax Press, 1990).

PART TWO: SELF
CHAPTER 3: TUNING IN

[1]Franz Kafka, *The Great Wall of China: Reflections.*

[2]Akong Tulku Rinpoche, *Taming the Tiger: Tibetan Teachings on Right Conduct, Mindfulness and Universal Compassion* (Rochester, VT: Inner Traditions International, 1995). Akong Tulku Rinpoche is an accomplished meditation master of the Karma Kagyu lineage of Tibetan Buddhism. He came to the West in 1963 and together with Chögyam Trungpa Rinpoche founded the Kagyu Samyé Ling Tibetan Center in Scotland, the oldest Tibetan center in the West.

Akong Rinpoche is also a fully trained doctor in the Tibetan medical tradition.

[3]Jon Kabat-Zinn, *Full Catastrophe Living* (New York: Dell Publishing, 1990). Kabat-Zinn is the founder of the Stress Reduction and Relaxation Program at the University of Massachusetts Medical Center. People with a whole range of medical problems—from headaches, high blood pressure, and back pain to heart disease, cancer, and AIDS—have participated in and benefited from Kabat-Zinn's program.

[4]Chögyam Trungpa Rinpoche, *The Path Is the Goal* (Boston: Shambhala Publications, 1995).

[5]This story is paraphrased from the Majjhima Nikāya, number 10, one of the oldest records of the historical Buddha's original teachings and authorized scripture of the Theravāda school of Buddhism. *The Middle Discourses of the Buddha,* translated by Bhikkhu Ñāmoli and Bhikkhu Bodhi (Boston: Wisdom Publications, 1995).

[6]This quote of Buddha's words is from Thich Nhat Hanh and Annabel Laity in *Transformation and Healing, Sutra on the Four Establishments of Mindfulness* (Berkeley, CA: Parallax Press, 1990). The source text is the Kayagatasati Sutra on mindfulness in the body in the Majjhima Nikāya, The Middle Discourses of the Buddha.

CHAPTER 4: NAMING YOUR EXPERIENCE

[1]Zen Master Dōgen, from "Tenzo Kyōkun" (Instructions for the Zen Cook), an essay regarding the rules and manner of the Zen kitchen. The version presented here is from Dōgen and Uchiyama, *Refining Your Life,* translated by Thomas Wright (New York: Weatherhill Press, 1983).

Eihei Dōgen (1200–1253) brought the Chinese practice of Zen—sometimes described as mindfulness concentration in serenity, a single-minded sitting meditation where one does not try to solve questions or attain realization—to Japan and, through his writings, now to the West. Dōgen Zenji is considered one of the greatest religious teachers of Japan. He was a poet, mystic, and philosopher, compiling many of his major works while in his thirties.

[2]Daniel Goleman, *Working with Emotional Intelligence* (New York: Bantam Books, 1998).

[3]John Gottman, *The Heart of Parenting* (New York: Simon & Schuster, 1997).

[4]Georgei Ivanovitch Gurdjieff (circa 1866–1949), as quoted by Akong Tulku Rinpoche in *Taming the Tiger* (Rochester, VT: Inner Traditions International, 1995).

[5]Daniel Goleman, *Emotional Intelligence* (New York: Bantam Books, 1997).

[6]Pamphlet on Jesuit spirituality, http://www.stignatiussf. org/jesuit_spirituality_1.htm.

[7]*Ibid.*

[8]Thich Nhat Hanh, *Peace Is Every Step* (New York: Bantam Books, 1991).

[9]Thich Nhat Hanh and Annabel Laity, *Transformation and Healing, Sutra on the Four Establishments of Mindfulness* (Berkeley, CA: Parallax Press, 1990).

[10]The term *dharma heir* refers to a student who has been given an acknowledgment of mastery and entrustment of knowledge by his or her Buddhist teacher. This transmission has remained unchanged throughout all generations of those who follow the teachings of Shakyamuni Buddha, have attained a spiritual awakening, and teach others. In this case Dosho Port-sensei was given dharma transmission by his teacher, Dainin Katagiri-roshi, and is, therefore, considered to be one of Katagiri's dharma heirs.

[11]Dainin Katagiri (1928–1990) was a central figure in transmitting Buddhism to America. In Japan he studied at Eiheiji Monastery and attended Komazawa University. In 1963, he came to the Zenshuji Soto Mission School in Los Angeles and then moved to assist Shunryu Suzuki Roshi at the San Francisco Zen Center. In 1972, he became the first abbot of the Minnesota Zen Meditation Center in Minneapolis, Minnesota. Katagiri-roshi died in 1990.

CHAPTER 5: ACCEPTING WHAT YOU FEEL

[1]Teresa of Avila was a sixteenth-century Spanish-born Carmelite nun who lived and wrote during the Counter-Reformation in Spain, under the shadow of the Inquisition. Teresa's mission—the founding of strict and enclosed monasteries—satisfied her longing to be actively involved in reforming religious life.

[2]Thich Nhat Hanh and Annabel Laity, *Transformation and Healing, Sutra on the Four Establishments of Mindfulness* (Berkeley, CA: Parallax Press, 1990).

CHAPTER 6: LOOKING DEEPLY

[1]As quoted in the foreword of *Mind in Buddhist Psychology,* translated from Tibetan by Herbert V. Guenther and Leslie S. Kawamura (Emeryville, CA: Dharma Publishing, 1975). From a translation of *The Necklace of Clear Understanding* by Ye-Shes Rgyal-Mtshan (1713–1793). Tarthang Tulku Rinpoche is head Lama of the Tibetan Nyingma Meditation Center and the Nyingma Institute, Berkeley, California.

[2]Mental formations as the root of feeling: Thich Nhat Hanh and Annabel Laity, *Transformation and Healing, Sutra on the Four Establishments of Mindfulness* (Berkeley, CA: Parallax Press, 1990).

[3]Lie Zi, *100 Allegorical Tales from Traditional China,* rewritten by Wei Jinzhi and translated by Jan and Yvonne Walls (Hong Kong: Joint Publishing Company, 1982).

Allegorical tales first flourished in China during the fifth to third centuries B.C.E. The influence of the allegorical tales, especially of the early ones, is twofold. The pre-Qin (Qin, 221–27 B.C.E.) allegorical tales represent the earliest satirical prose in China. They marked the beginning of a whole genre of satirical writing, especially fiction, in the historical development of Chinese literature.

The other influence is in language. These terse and concise stories have become so popular and well known that many of them have simply become part of the Chinese language as idiomatic sayings. This tale has been selected and translated from a collection called *Zhongguo Gudai Yuyan*, edited and rendered into *baihua* by the modern writer Wei Jinzhi (1900–1972). The tales provide enjoyment as well as insights into some of the more famous traditional Chinese conceptions of incongruity in human behavior.

[4]Study by Burns and Seligman, 1989, as reported in *Learned Optimism* (New York: Simon & Schuster, 1990).

[5]Mind and Life Institute, edited by Daniel Goleman, *Healing Emotions: Conversations with the Dalai Lama on Mindfulness, Emotions and Health* (Boston: Shambhala Publications, 1997).

[6]Mind and Life Institute, *op. cit.*

[7]Study by Gary Schwartz and colleagues at Harvard, Mind and Life Institute, *op. cit.*

[8]Chögyam Trungpa Rinpoche, *The Path Is the Goal* (Boston: Shambhala Publications, 1995).

[9]This list of the signs of strong anger is adapted from the work of Robert Mann and Rose Youd, *Buddhist Character Analysis* (Avon, UK: Aukuna Trust, 1992).

[10]Anger consumes our self-control: Thich Nhat Hanh and Annabel Laity, *op. cit.*

[11]This list of the signs of craving is adapted from the work of Robert Mann and Rose Youd, *op. cit.*

[12]Tsongkhapa is the founder of the Gelugpa sect in Tibet. He is considered an incarnation of Mañjughosa, a Tibetan representation of discriminating awareness and the inspiration for true understanding. He holds the flame sword of discrimination in his right hand and the book of knowledge in his left.

From *Necklace of Clear Understanding: An Elucidation of the Workings of the Mind and Mental Events,* by Ye-Shes Rgyal-Mtshan (1713–1793) translated from Tibetan by Guenther and Kawamura, *Mind in Buddhist Psychology* (Emeryville, CA: Dharma Publishing, 1975).

[13]This list of the signs of delusion is adapted from the work of Robert Mann and Rose Youd, *op. cit.*

[14]Akong Tulku Rinpoche, *Taming the Tiger: Tibetan Teachings on Right Conduct, Mindfulness and Universal Compassion* (Rochester, VT: Inner Traditions International, 1995).

CHAPTER 7: STAYING POISED

[1]Daniel Goleman, *Emotional Intelligence* (New York: Bantam Books, 1995).

[2]Daniel Goleman, *Working with Emotional Intelligence* (New York: Bantam Books, 1998).

[3]Daniel Goleman, Richard Boyatzis, and Annie McKee, *Primal Leadership* (Boston: Harvard Business Review Press, 2002).

[4]Robert Ornstein, *The Evolution of Consciousness* (New York: Simon & Schuster, 1991).

[5]Cameron Carter, Angus Macdonald, Stefan Ursu, Andy Stenger, Myeong Ho Sohn, and John Anderson, "How the Brain Gets Ready to Perform" (presentation at the 30th annual meeting of the Society of Neuroscience, New Orleans, November 2000). As reported in Daniel Goleman et al., *op. cit.*

[6]Cliff Saron and Richard J. Davidson in "The Brain and Emotions," *Healing Emotions: Conversations with the Dalai Lama on Mindfulness, Emotions, and Health,* edited by Daniel Goleman (Boston: Shambhala Publications, 1997).

[7]Changing habits: Goleman et al., *op. cit.*

[8]Portia Nelson, as quoted in Charles L. Whitfield, *Healing the Child Within* (Orlando, FL: Health Communications, 1989).

[9]Cliff Saron and Richard J. Davidson, *op. cit.*

[10]This meditation is drawn from koan number 18 in *The Blue Cliff Record: The National Teacher Chung's Seamless Monument* (Boston: Shambhala Publications, 1992).

The Blue Cliff Record has become almost uniquely revered among Zen Buddhists as a model koan text, especially noted for its subtlety and profundity in both form and content.

Koan number 18, as translated by Thomas Cleary and J. C. Cleary, reads:

My late teacher Wu Tsu brought up the "Seamless Monument" and said, "In front it is pearls and agate, in back agate and pearls; on the east are Avalokitesvara and Mahasthamaprapta, on the west are Manjusri and Samantabhadra; in the middle there's a flag blown by the wind, saying, Flap, flap."

[11]*Koan* literally means "public document." It refers to a record of seventeen hundred traditional citations and stories, representing the "official" body of Zen lore. These vignettes, known as *gongan* in Chinese and *koan* in Japanese and English, are intended to foster specific perceptions and insights that penetrate the mind. Meditation on a koan is believed to transcend the intellect, allowing the student to experience the true nature of reality.

[12]Tantric teachings have among their foundations the oldest teachings known. In Eastern tradition, Tantric practice is part of the Vajrayana school and makes use of yoga, visualizations, mantras (mystical invocations), mudras (symbolic body posture or hand gestures), mandalas (symbolic diagrams), and other rituals.

A mantra is a mystical invocation used in some Buddhist schools, including the Shingon school in Japan and Tantric Buddhism in Tibet. The word *mantra* literally means "mind protection." The sounds of the mantras, not the meanings, are the basis for their mystical power. A mudra is a symbolic body posture or hand gesture. Its power lies in the actual posture itself as a means to communicate the quality of truth.

[13]This conclusion is presented by Angeles Arrien, an anthropologist, author, and educator, in *The Four-Fold Way: Walking the Paths of the Warrior, Teacher, Healer and Visionary* (San Francisco: HarperSanFrancisco, 1993).

[14]Types of visualizations: a reference to the work of Ira Pro-

goff, *The Symbolic and the Real* (New York: McGraw-Hill, 1963).

[15]According to Taigen Daniel Leighton in his book *Bodhisattva Archetypes* (New York: Penguin Books, 1998), images of bodhisattvas are fundamentally understood as representations of awakened qualities within our own selves, and within all beings.

[16]Errol Korn and Karen Johnson, in *Visualization: The Uses of Imagery in the Health Professions* (Homewood, IL: Dorsey Professional Series, Dow Jones–Irwin, 1983).

[17]In modern times, Tantra remains as a living tradition only among Tibetan people—or at least this was so until the Chinese communist invasion—although strong remnants continue in areas of India and Japan.

[18]The Venerable Thrangu Rinpoche is one of the foremost teachers of the Kagyu tradition. He holds a degree of Geshe Rabjam, the highest scholarship degree in the four sects of Tibetan Buddhism, and is recognized as a master of the Mahamudra teachings. Thrangu Rinpoche is renowned for his ability to make the most profound dharma teachings easily accessible to Western students at all levels.

[19]Akong Tulku Rinpoche, *Taming the Tiger: Tibetan Teachings on Right Conduct, Mindfulness and Universal Compassion* (Rochester, VT: Inner Traditions International, 1995).

This description of Visualizing Blue-Black Light to Counteract Anger is taken from Akong Rinpoche's teachings at the Kagyu Samyé Ling Tibetan Center in Scotland, the oldest Tibetan center in the West. Dr. Akong Tulku Rinpoche is an accomplished meditation master of the Karma Kagyu lineage of Tibetan Buddhism. The spiritual director of Samyé Ling and the founder of other centers in Europe, Asia, and Africa, Akong Rinpoche is also a fully trained doctor in the Tibetan medical tradition and the leader of several humanitarian organizations.

[20]Dōgen Zenji, from the *Zazanshin* (The Acupuncture Needle of Zazen) fascicle of the thirteenth-century text

Shobogenzo in *Dōgen's Manuals of Zen Meditation* by Carl Bielefeldt.

[21]The Mountain Meditation was introduced to the West by Thich Nhat Hanh and popularized by Jon Kabat-Zinn and the Stress Reduction and Mindfulness Clinic in Massachusetts.

[22]Jon Kabat-Zinn, *Wherever You Go, There You Are: Mindfulness Meditation in Everyday Life* (New York: Hyperion, 1994).

PART THREE: OTHER
CHAPTER 8: DEEPENING EMPATHY

[1]Abraham Lincoln, in his first inaugural address, March 4, 1861.

[2]The source text for this quote is the Hua-yen Sutra, as taught by Tu-shun (557–640), the first patriarch of the Hua-yen school of Chinese Buddhism. He is remembered as a monk with exceptional healing abilities and someone who lived close to the peasants in his time. This translation is by Thomas Cleary and appears in Stephanie Kaza and Kenneth Kraft, *Dharma Rain: Sources of Buddhist Environmentalism* (Boston: Shambhala Publications, 2000).

[3]Larry Dossey, *Prayer Is Good Medicine: How to Reap the Healing Benefits of Prayer* (San Francisco: HarperSanFrancisco, 1996).

[4]I owe my understanding of sociobiology, superorganism theory, and complexity theory to a series of conversations with Scott Smith and several books: *The Global Brain* and *The Lucifer Principle*, by Howard Bloom; *Emergence*, by Steven Johnson; *Non-Zero*, by Robert Wright; *What Is Life?* and *Symbiotic Planet*, by Lynn Margulis and Dorion Sagan; and *Sociobiology*, by Edward O. Wilson.

[5]Lewis Thomas, *Lives of a Cell: Notes of a Biology Watcher* (New York: Bantam Books, 1974).

[6]Thich Nhat Hanh, *Peace Is Every Step* (New York: Bantam Books, 1991).

[7]Daniel Goleman, *Working with Emotional Intelligence* (New York: Bantam Books, 1998).

[8]This research cited in Daniel Goleman, Richard Boyatzis, and Annie McKee, *Primal Leadership: The Hidden Driver of Great Performance* (Boston: Harvard Business Review Press, 2001).

[9]Larry Dossey, *op. cit.*

[10]The Dalai Lama, *A Flash of Lightning in the Dark of Night* (Boston: Shambhala Publications, 1994).

[11]The effect of good thoughts: The Dalai Lama, *The Art of Happiness: A Handbook for Living* (New York: Riverhead Books, 1998).

[12]The importance of empathy: *ibid.*

[13]Geshe Rabten and Geshe Ngawang Dhargyey, *Advice from a Spiritual Friend*, rev. ed., translated and edited by Brian Beresford with Gonsar Tulku and Sherpa Tulku (London: Wisdom Publications, 1984). They are discussing a quote from Shantideva's *Guide to the Bodhisattva's Way of Life:* "The awakened mind is like a diamond, the sun and the healing tree."

[14]Walking in another person's shoes: The Dalai Lama, *op. cit.*

CHAPTER 9: LIVING IN HARMONY

[1]John Daido Loori, *The Eight Gates of Zen* (New York: Dharma Communications, Zen Mountain Monastery, 1992). John Daido Loori is the spiritual leader and abbot of Zen Mountain Monastery in Mount Tremper, New York, and the founder and director of the Mountains and Rivers Order, an organization of associated Zen Buddhist temples, practice centers, and sitting groups in the United States and abroad. He is an authenticated lineage holder, trained in the rigorous school of koan Zen.

[2]Sharon Salzberg, *Lovingkindness: The Revolutionary Art of Happiness* (Boston: Shambhala Publications, 1995). These

words are her translation of Gautama Buddha's Metta Sutta, or discourse on loving-kindness.

[3]John Daido Loori, *op. cit.*

[4]Dainin Katagiri, *Returning to Silence: Zen Practice in Daily Life* (Boston: Shambhala Publications, 1988).

[5]Rough language: Dainin Katagiri, *op.cit.*

[6]Dōgen Zenji, *Moon in a Dewdrop* (San Francisco: San Francisco Zen Center, 1985). This quote is from Dōgen's *Shōbōgenzo*, the *Bodhisattva's Four Methods of Guidance,* which was written in 1243, primarily for lay students of Buddhism. Bodhisattva is a Sanskrit word meaning a heroic being or spiritual warrior who is committed to the path of compassion.

[7]Daniel Goleman, Richard Boyatzis, and Annie McKee, *Primal Leadership: The Hidden Driver of Great Performance* (Boston: Harvard Business Review Press, 2001).

[8]Work teams share moods: Research reported by Goleman et al., *op. cit.*

[9]Kind speech turning the destiny of nations: Dōgen Zenji, *op. cit.*

[10]Diane Tice and Roy F. Baumeister, "Controlling Anger: Self-Induced Emotions Change," in Wegner and Pennebaker, *Handbook of Mental Control;* also Carol Tavris, *Anger: The Misunderstood Emotion* (New York: Touchstone, 1989), as reported in Daniel Goleman's *Emotional Intelligence* (New York: Bantam Books, 1995).

[11]Daniel Goleman, *op. cit.*

[12]Studies by Dr. Zillman are reported in "Mental Control of Angry Aggression," in Wegner and Pennebaker, *Handbook of Mental Control,* cited in Daniel Goleman, *op. cit.*

[13]Rage erupting into violence: Daniel Goleman, *op. cit.*

[14]The Dalai Lama, *Healing Anger: The Power of Patience from a Buddhist Perspective,* translated by Geshe Thupten Jinpa (New York: Snow Lion Publications, 1997).

[15]Written in the eighth century B.C.E., Shantideva's Guide to the Bodhisattva's Way of Life soon became a classic of Mahayana Buddhism. Legend has it that Shantideva recited

the entire text extemporaneously when he was asked to give a lecture to a congregation of monks at the famous Indian monastic university of Nalanda.

It is said that the request to teach initially arose out of a desire to humiliate Shantideva, whom his fellow monks saw as doing nothing, referring to him as the "eat-sleep-and-shit monk." Little did the monks realize that while Shantideva appeared to be leading a somewhat lazy life, he was in fact rich in inner experience and profound learning. Tibetan accounts of the story maintain that when Shantideva reached the difficult ninth chapter, the chapter on wisdom, he started to ascend into the air and began to disappear, although his voice could still be heard.

[16]The practice of Visualizing the Effects of Strong Anger is adapted from the Dalai Lama, *op. cit.*

[17]This gatha is taken from the Dhammapada, a collection of the original sayings of Buddha Shakyamuni, chapter 1, verses 5–6. In a translation of the original text by Ekanth Easwaran, these verses read:

> For hatred can never put an end to hatred, love alone can. This is the unalterable law.

[18]Authors of this document were Dosho Port-sensei, Byakuren Judith Ragir, Ruth Elaine Hane, Keith Rodli, Robert Zeglovitch, and Thérèse Jacobs-Stewart, from Clouds in Water Zen Center in St. Paul, Minnesota.

[19]Many times the very process of understanding becomes the solution itself, but at times we need to go on to negotiating further actions for the future.

[20]Thich Nhat Hanh, *Peace Is Every Step* (New York: Bantam Books, 1991).

[21]From teachings by the Indian master Shantideva, in Guide to the Bodhisattva's Way of Life (Bodicaryavatara), chapter 6, verses 106–107, eighth century B.C.E.

[22]Taking strong countermeasures: The Dalai Lama, *The Art*

of Happiness: A Handbook for Living (New York: Riverhead Books, 1998).

[23]These examples of setting limits are adapted from Paul Mason and Randi Kreger, *Stop Walking on Eggshells* (Oakland, CA: New Harbinger Publications, 1998).

[24]*Ibid.*

CHAPTER 10: LETTING GO

[1]Heraclitus, from Diogenes Laertius, Lives of Eminent Philosophers, book 9, section 8; and Plato, Cratylus, 402A.

[2]Gautama Buddha, as cited in Sharon Salzberg, *Lovingkindness: The Revolutionary Art of Happiness* (Boston: Shambhala Publications, 1995).

[3]This is the last verse from the Buddhist Sutra The Diamond That Cuts Through Illusion.

[4]The Four Sublime Attitudes are collectively termed the Brahma-Vihara from the *Tevijja Sutta* in *The Long Discourses on Buddha: A Translation of the Digha Nikaya* by Maurice Walshe (Somerville, MA: Wisdom Publications, 1995).

[5]Adapted from Pamela Bloom, *Buddhist Acts of Compassion* (Berkeley, CA: Conari Press, 2000).

[6]From the Buddha's teachings on the Divine Abidings and Their Perfection (Brahma-vihara) translated by Bhikku Khantipalo, "Practical Advice for Meditators," *The Wheel Publication No. 116* (Kandy, Sri Lanka: Buddhist Publication Society, 1986).

[7]*Ibid.*

[8]Bhikkhu Khantipalo also says: "The mind well-practiced in these four virtues, and then well-trained by their use in daily life, has already gained very much."

[9]Shantideva, in Guide to the Bodhisattva's Way of Life (Bodicaryavatara). In a translation of the original text by Vesna A. Wallace and B. Alan Wallace, this verse reads:

If it can be remedied, why worry? If it cannot be remedied, why worry?

[10]Sharon Salzberg, *op. cit.*

[11]This oral tale is adapted from the version found on John Suler's Web site at www.rider.edu., *Zen Stories to Tell Your Neighbors*

[12]This is the last line of The Five Remembrances, a Buddhist gatha presented by Yvonne Rand in the Arising and Vanishing retreat at Clouds in Water Zen Center, February 1999. The entire text of The Five Remembrances is as follows:

> *I am of the nature to grow old, there is no escaping growing old.*
> *I am of the nature to have ill health, there is no way to avoid ill health.*
> *I am of the nature to die, there is no way to avoid death.*
> *All that is dear to me and everyone that I love is of the nature to change; there is no way to avoid being separated from them.*
> *My deeds are my closest companions. I am the beneficiary of my deeds. My deeds are the best representation of who I am.*

[13]A description of Equanimity Practice, Sharon Salzberg, *op. cit.*

[14]These instructions for Meditating with Equanimity Phrases are adapted from *ibid.*

[15]Larry Dossey, *Prayer Is Good Medicine: How to Reap the Healing Benefits of Prayer* (San Francisco: HarperSanFrancisco, 1996).

[16]Impassiveness when practicing equanimity: Sharon Salzberg, *op. cit.*

[17]This Buddhist gatha for developing equanimity is from Bhikkhu Khantipalo, *op. cit.*

PARTING WORDS

[1]Antonio Machado, *Proverbios y Cantares* (Proverbs and Songs), 29 in *Selected Poems of Antonio Machado*, translated by

Betty Jean Craige, University of Georgia (Baton Rouge: Louisiana State University Press, 1979).

[2]Heraclitus, *On the Universe,* fragment 1. Translated by W. H. S. Jones.

APPENDIX

[1]These exemplars of bodhisattva characteristics are taken from Taigen Daniel Leighton, *Bodhisattva Archetypes* (New York: Penguin Books, 1998).

[2]The descriptions of these Old Testament figures are adapted from *The Oxford Companion to the Bible,* edited by Bruce Metzger and Michael Coogan (New York: Oxford University Press, 1993). My thanks to Marilyn Habermas-Scher and Diane Elliot for their consultation regarding wisdom figures in the Jewish tradition.

[3]The descriptions of these New Testament figures are adapted from *ibid.*

[4]These portrayals of indigenous archetypes are presented by Angeles Arrien, an anthropologist, author, and educator, in *The Four-Fold Way: Walking the Paths of the Warrior, Teacher, Healer and Visionary* (San Francisco: HarperSanFrancisco, 1993).

FOR MORE INFORMATION

For information about seminars and retreats on
Paths Are Made by Walking:

www.mindroads.com